The Oracy Instructional Guide

*Linking Research and Theory
to Assessment and Instruction*

Pre K-3

Developed and Written by Lance M. Gentile, Ph.D.

DOMINIE PRESS
Pearson Learning Group

Dedicated to Mary A. Gentile and Merna M. McMillan Ph.D. for a life's worth of personal and professional editorial work on my behalf; with special thanks to Merna for the painstaking support she provided me in creating this version of the The Oracy Instructional Guide.

Lance M. Gentile

ISBN 0-7685-2301-X
Printed in Singapore
3 4 5 6   09 08 07 06 05

Dominie Press
Pearson Learning Group

1-800-321-3106
www.pearsonlearning.com

Table of Contents

Introduction

"It's powerful to harness the established power of children's oral language to literacy learning from the beginning, so that new literacy knowledge and new oral language powers are linked and patterned from the start. Children with the least preparation for literacy learning need such an integrated approach if they are to catch up to their classmates."

M. Clay

The Oracy Instructional Guide provides teachers key information and ways to use *The Oral Language Acquisition Inventory* (OLAI) to help English Language Learners (ELL) and children with low oral language development achieve literacy and stay in school.

The OLAI is used for teaching and ongoing assessment to monitor learning and shape instruction for these Hard to Reach Hard to Teach children.

Results of the OLAI can be used for classroom instruction to:

1. Guide and focus interactions to increase opportunities for children to talk about text.

2. Design specific prompts to help children expand and refine oral language production, enhancing the ability to read and write for meaning.

3. Match reading and writing experiences with text that contains the language structures and vocabulary children control or are beginning to control.

4. Group children in regular classrooms for daily intervention to afford them opportunities to catch up with their peers.

5. Provide a baseline and ongoing measurement of growth in language and literacy development.

6. Supplement other oral language and literacy programs and measurements.

It is critical to assess language development and link the results to reading and writing instruction because:

1. There is a rapid increase in the number of preschool/school-age children whose lack of language development interferes with their ability to learn to read and write and succeed in school. It is estimated that at least 40 percent of these children fail to reach acceptable levels of English reading and writing by the end of elementary school. For older English Language Learners (ELLs) and children with limited language development, failure to reach grade level competence persists and contributes to

their high dropout rate (Loban, 1976; Thomas and Collier, 1997).

2. Many children live in poverty, are isolated and enter school with limited life and language experiences. They may not have attended preschool and do not possess the concepts and vocabulary needed to even formulate complete sentences. This is true not only for English Language Learners but for those whose primary language is English as well (Healy, 1991).

> **Healy (1999, p. 232) said:**
>
> *Talk bridges the gap between a child's concrete, sensorial world and the world of images and abstract concepts; thus it teaches "representational distance," so important for learning to think about symbols and things that aren't immediately present (as in math concepts, or reading comprehension). To expect children to become literate before they have a basis of language understanding is an exercise in futility. They may learn to sound out words, but that's where the story ends.*

3. Children from second-language backgrounds or those who struggle with language development frequently receive excessive drill-and-skill instruction and little if any specific, integrated language and literacy instruction (see Figure 1, Page 2). This happens because the training of many teachers is confined to these methods or because it is imposed on them in the form of mandated tests, materials and programs that do not meet the needs of these children (Kohn, 1999).

4. The literacy instructional curriculum is driven by what is tested.

Language is a major factor in brain development as well as in achieving literacy (Pinker, 1994). "Language shapes culture, language shapes thinking and language shapes brains" (Healy, 1991). Moreover, parts of the brain that get the most use expand and rewire on demand (Schwartz and Begley, 2002).

Talk is the cornerstone of language and literacy development, and it must be practiced. But children acquire a great deal of language indirectly as well as through direct instruction (National Reading Panel Report, 2000; Brabham and Villaume, 2002).

> **Luria (1968, p.85) said:**
>
> *Language is not only a means of generalization; it is at the same time the source of thought. When the child masters language he gains the potentiality to organize anew his perception, his memory; he masters more complex forms of reflection of objects in the external world; he gains the capacity to draw conclusions from his observations, to make deductions, the potentiality of thinking.*

For children to reach the level of cognitive growth necessary for reading and writing, they need daily opportunities for "interactive talk" before they start school and in school: talk with parents or caregivers, talk with teachers and other adults and talk with other children (Healy, 1999).

Children who lack these opportunities will need *systemic intervention* (see Figure 2, Page 2) to avoid dropping out of school or being pushed out because of basic reading and writing difficulties (Ralph, 1988).

Traditional instruction has failed to address the needs of many ELLs and low language children and continues to be a barrier to their learning (Grant and Wong, 2003). An Oracy Instructional Curriculum (OIC) provides *systemic intervention* that is different from traditional approaches. It is ongoing in every classroom across the grades. Oracy instruction links language development and literacy learning by emphasizing more powerful teacher-child interactions.

The optimum implementation of an OIC is described in Chapter 10, "Oracy Instruction: The Role of the School Administrator." If a school-wide effort is not possible, a learning environment emphasizing language acquisition and literacy instruction can still be developed one classroom at a time.

An OIC based on shared language and literacy learning experiences makes a difference in the way children are taught and the way they learn in school. This is critical because as Clay (1998, p. 208) said:

Oral language must be extended at a fast pace, otherwise children's entry competence may limit what they are able to make of all the subsequent opportunities provided by the education system. For want of a boost to oral language development a child could be lost to education.

The instructional blocks of a balanced literacy curriculum can support all children's literacy learning. For ELL children and those with low language development the challenge is not just to teach reading and writing explicitly but to link language and literacy instruction. A heavy emphasis on daily oral language activities is critical to their development as readers and writers. Gaining control of the most common language structures as well as a wide range of vocabulary and concepts to develop fluency and comprehension are the keys to learning.

Ideally, for children acquiring a second language the material to be taught is modeled in their first language; then they are provided with the second language translation. Wells, (1977, p. 9) said: "Talk is central to learning. Through talk we clarify our own understandings. Through talk we negotiate the construction of shared meanings."

Hanf-Buckley (1992, p.623) quoted a definitive statement from Walter Loban that forms the basis of an Oracy Instructional Curriculum:

Please, in the name of all that is good in language and thinking, please let the children talk. Let them talk a great deal; listen to the equivalent of a book a day; talk the equivalent of a book a week; read the equivalent of a book a month and write the equivalent of book a year.

1 Closing the Gap
Systemic Intervention for Stages I and II Children

"When you're navigating by the wrong stars, pulling harder on the oars still won't get you to your destination."

C. Finn

Many children who are acquiring English as a second language or whose oral language development lags cannot interact with teachers and texts to demonstrate expected levels of learning. They cannot perform well on mandated tests and are always behind struggling to catch up. The tendency to add more pages or time spent on skill building practice materials without changing the approach only compounds the problem (NCLB, 2000).

You can play a vital role in redesigning traditional reading and writing instruction for the lowest performing children without compromising the quality of instruction in the classroom. These children can be included in the instructional conversation instead of being left sitting on the sidelines, watching while the game goes on without them, the gap widening between their level of performance and that of higher achieving children (Stevens, 2003).

Inevitably, children with low oral language development and those acquiring a second language may be frustrated, angry or depressed because they are unable to benefit from whole class, traditional instruction (Gentile and McMillan, 1990, 1991).

They cannot do what other children who control the language of instruction can do. Soon they are not *left behind*; they are *left out*—out of sorts, out of the instructional conversation, out of the curriculum and eventually out of school before graduation. They and their parents wonder what's wrong with them. Why can't they succeed the way other children do? In traditional classroom instruction the curriculum of the language arts is devoted to teaching literacy, i.e., reading and writing. Teachers' interactions with children are centered on text. Language development is wrongly assumed to occur naturally, over time, without an explicit emphasis in the curriculum (see Figure 1, Page 2).

The challenge is to make the time and resources available to provide Stages I and II children 30 minutes of daily Oracy instruction in a small group and organize three or four independent, cooperative language and literacy centers (Blakemore and Ramirez, 1999).

"I've sawed this board off three times and it's still too short."

Traditional instruction contributes to an achievement gap that has not narrowed in more than a decade, despite an increasing emphasis on reading and writing skills development (Stevens, 2003). This approach treats oral language as an assumed curriculum so it may be overlooked or left out. The instructional interactions are focused on reading and writing text contained in commercially published materials, even though teachers are working in *language* arts programs. Spending more time doing the same thing has never and will never narrow the gap.

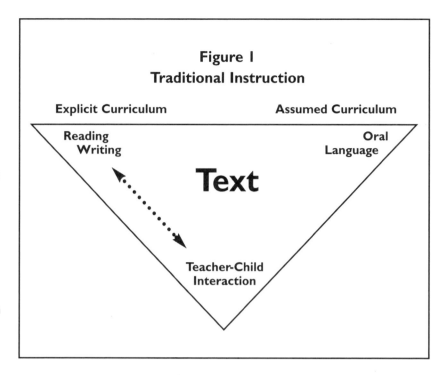

Figure 1
Traditional Instruction

Explicit Curriculum — Assumed Curriculum
Reading Writing — Oral Language
Text
Teacher-Child Interaction

"If you expect a different result you have to change what you are doing."

Systemic intervention links language and literacy instruction across the grades, creating an OIC. This approach contains a dual, explicit focus, combining *talk* and *text* with meaningful listening, speaking, reading, writing and viewing instructional interactions. The OIC does not require purchasing new programs or materials but relies on teachers learning to reorganize the classroom, use materials already available in the school and interact differently with the lowest performing children.

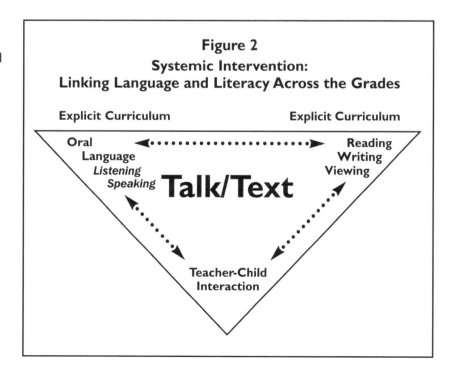

Figure 2
Systemic Intervention:
Linking Language and Literacy Across the Grades

Explicit Curriculum — Explicit Curriculum
Oral Language *Listening Speaking* — Reading Writing Viewing
Talk/Text
Teacher-Child Interaction

2 Oracy Instruction for Stages I and II Children in Regular Classrooms

"Reading and writing float on a sea of talk."

J. Britton

By working each day to develop Oracy instruction, you can become a more effective literacy teacher for struggling language learners. The steps are:

1. Make individual assessments of the lowest performing children's oral language acquisition, using the OLAI.

2. Plan and teach a daily lesson for 30 minutes to a group of four children using the results and components of the OLAI to guide instruction and shape your interactions.

3. Design lessons using the Four Blocks of an OIC following a theme for several days (see Figure 3).

4. Evaluate your lesson. What worked well? What needs repeating or more emphasis? What needs to be changed?

5. Request objective observation and comment from a knowledgeable colleague.

6. Plan and teach the next lesson, using what you learned.

7. Take every opportunity to restate, expand and refine children's language. As difficult as it may be, find occasions to laugh and enjoy working with the lowest performing children. You are making a difference. Remember, a lesson without laughter is a lesson lost.

Figure 3 An OIC for Children in Regular Classrooms: Four Blocks of Instruction	
1. Activity (Creative Arts/Puzzles) • *Talk* about what you'll do. • Do it and *talk* while doing it, when it's appropriate. • *Talk* about what you did.	**2. Reading** • *Talk* about what you'll read. • Read and *talk* during the reading, when it's appropriate, • *Talk* about what you read.
3. Writing • *Talk* about what you'll write. • Write and *talk* during the writing, when it's appropriate. • *Talk* about what you wrote.	**4. Viewing and Listening** • *Talk* about what you'll watch or hear. • Watch or listen and *talk* during the selected segment of video or audiotape, when it's appropriate. • *Talk* about what you watched or heard.

Organizing for Instruction

You can divide your classroom for 30 minutes each day providing *four* Stage I and II language users intense Oracy instruction while other groups work at separate, meaningful language and literacy learning centers. This allows you the time to work with these children without compromising or diluting the others' learning.

Four has proven to be the optimal number because it allows you to retain your focus, intensify interactions with the lowest performing children and provide opportunities for them to interact with each other as well as with you, i.e., *pair, share, think* and *talk* (PSTT).

Reorganizing a traditional classroom in this way is strengthened in grades 1-3 through the help of a volunteer-parent, relative, other adult or older tutor. In preschool or kindergarten, if children are to do more than "busy" work in centers a support person is *required* to successfully manage classrooms.

If you use an aide, volunteer or tutor to help you manage the language and literacy learning activities at separate centers, they need to be trained to function as autonomously as possible so your work with the Oracy group is not interrupted.

The time the other children spend away from you should not be relegated solely to paper and pencil, fill-in-the-blank ditto sheets (Ford, 1991).

The next chapter describes ten different ways to furnish children meaningful language and literacy learning experiences at different centers.

Location
Arrange a table and chairs in the room so you can observe and help monitor the rest of the class working at independent, cooperative language and literacy learning centers.

Time Required
Approximately thirty minutes daily. These activities can be unique each day or follow a theme over time.

Materials Needed
Big Books/Wordless Books, easel, pointer, chalkboard or whiteboard, chalk, markers, erasers, felt board and felt-backed story frame pictures, magnetic boards, magnetic letters, trays, pocket charts, blank sentence strips, freezer bags, chart tablets, writing and drawing materials, notebooks, expository texts as well as storybooks, newspapers, magazines, large picture posters, audio and videotapes, a tape recorder, VCR and monitor.

Shared Activities
Organize hands-on activities that can be completed in 5-10 minutes. Children can help select from a wide range of topics related to subject area concepts and other interests. You may also read and talk with children, or draw, write and talk with them. They can also PSTT doing the same things or engage in follow-up language and literacy learning.

Goals
*   To intensify your interactions with the lowest performing children in language and literacy and provide effective, daily intervention.

*   To establish structured, predictable routines and differentiated opportunities for active participation that encourage children to work together as well as with you.

Directions
*   Each day make or do something to familiarize children with an object, topic, concept or experience. Ask them what they know about it and invite responses.

- *Talk* with the children and facilitate the conversation. Restate, clarify, expand and refine their responses. Solicit what more they would like to know.

- Then read and think aloud or tell a story, provide pictures or photos or present a brief audio or videotape segment that clarifies or expands what the children know. Afterward, ask what more the children have learned from these additional experiences and *talk* with them.

- Have the children make or do something (PSTT) based on what they knew originally, what they learned from your read and think aloud, storytelling, pictures, photos, audio or video segment.

- Ask the children to say something about what they have made or done and compose a dictation chart that contains one response from each child. This chart forms the text for guided or independent reading and writing and recording progress, i.e., Running Records or other individualized assessments.

- Read the chart aloud to the group, pointing at each word while the children "read" along silently.

- Then read the chart aloud together, following the same procedure. One child may be invited to do the pointing and reading of a single line of text or a complete chart as you and the other children follow along.

- Highlight high frequency or multi-syllabic words in the chart and model using whole word, sound-letter, i.e., phonemic analysis or onset and rime word identification strategies.

- Invite the children individually to construct these words on a large magnetic board placed in front of the group.

- Then ask the children to identify a favorite word from the chart. They will use that word when learning how to construct words.

- Provide each pair of children one tray containing letters of a word they or you selected from the dictation chart. Ask them to work together and *talk* as they arrange the letters in order to make the word.

- Encourage children to independently write one additional statement or response to the dictation chart in a writing notebook or journal. They may use invented spellings or cross-check the spellings of high frequency words using the chart or word wall.

- Move around the group to support the composition of their independent written responses and their spelling.

Children learn to write high frequency and favorite words as well as some common nouns and verbs as they independently compose a sentence or two about an object, topic or event related to instructional activities. They can collaborate (PSTT) and work with you to edit and illustrate their work for publication.

You can make a reading "book" for each child at the end of five days by generating computer copies of the edited sentences. These can be pasted over the handwritten ones to make word-perfect versions. The books can be used by you and the children to set purposes for guided or independent reading and writing activities.

3 Managing Independent Language and Literacy Learning Centers

"We can, with John Dewey, conceive of 'mind as a verb rather than a noun,' and can thereby be open to the possibility of attentiveness, engagement and action."

W. Ayers

Appropriate behaviors, procedures and goals in independent centers must be clearly established so children know exactly what they are expected to do and accomplish. The time spent in these centers should not be relegated to "busy work" or paper and pencil, fill-in-the-blank worksheets (Ford, 1991).

Centers work best if you:
- Establish three or four additional centers in the room.
- Station no more than 6 children at each center.
- Define roles and provide clear, consistent directions.
- Work with aides, volunteers or tutors to structure goals and outcomes for each center.
- Provide meaningful language and literacy learning activities for each center.
- When you have finished working with the Oracy instructional group, have each center briefly report on their work.
- Provide opportunities for aides, volunteers, tutors and children to give feedback. Redesign activities in response to their suggestions.

Ford and Opitz (2002, pp. 714-716) described the following nine activities that constitute meaningful language and literacy learning centers for children working away from the teacher. A tenth center, "Computer," has been added to this section.

1. Listening Post

This center provides children practice looking at print while listening to a story. Stories on tape and multiple copies of a text create opportunities for you to rotate children and materials. This allows children to prepare, review or go beyond a guided reading lesson. You are encouraged to hold children accountable by asking a member of the group to read or tell about one part of the story.

Pre/K children can use wordless picture books with an accompanying audiotaped narrative that signals them, at the appropriate time, to turn each page.

The authors identified a useful structure for expanding a listening post routine (p. 715):
- Listen to the story on tape and follow along.
- Listen to the story on tape and read along.
- Turn off the tape and read along.
- Turn off the tape and read with a partner.
- Listen to the story on tape and read with a partner.
- Turn off the tape and read on your own.

- Listen to the story on tape and read along again.
- Talk about your improvement.
- Be ready to share the story with the class.

2. Reader's Theater

A Reader's Theater center provides space, multiple copies of texts and a set of guidelines for practicing plays. This center can be used like Listening Post to warm up, review or go beyond what was done during guided reading. Children can be grouped more heterogeneously because different parts can be assigned to children based on their language and literacy strengths. Making simple props like masks and puppets using available materials builds children's motivation. The authors provide a Reader's Theater routine as well (p. 715).
- Leader reads the story aloud.
- Everyone reads the story together.
- Partners read the story together.
- Everyone is assigned a part.
- Children practice their parts on their own.
- Children practice their parts together.

Afterward, the children can be accountable for putting on their play for the class. Kane and Klein (1995, p. 5) said: "Oral language is a powerful way into written text and an equally powerful way of adding a new dimension to text by performing what is written to an audience of eager listeners."

3. Reading/Writing the Room

This center requires a print-rich, visually accessible environment that is changed regularly. Materials displayed can include large alphabet letters, important, difficult or colorful words and a word wall that contains multiple, alphabetically arranged high frequency words. The room also may display copies of children's story narratives or expository writing, their captioned drawings, messages and letters they have written, rules for the classroom, maps and illustrations related to content areas with accompanying texts, songs, and poetry. Large picture posters with subtitles or related text are also useful.

Photos of children and accompanying written interviews describing their families and pets, interests, activities or sports they like best, and favorite stories, movies, videos, songs and poems can appear on classroom walls as well.

Captioned drawings, messages and letters, classroom rules, maps and illustrations related to content areas with companion texts can be posted.

Children choose a partner and "read the room," using a pointer. They can use paper and pencil to catalog their favorite selections or record their responses to specific objectives related to this array of material (Neuman, Copple and Bredekamp, 2001).

Ford and Opitz (2002) provide a Scavenger Hunt routine that encourages children to explore concepts about print, letter names, word identification and vocabulary related to the classroom curriculum (p. 715):

Find three words in our room that:
- have more than six letters
- end in *-ing* where the final letter is doubled
- mean the same as *said*
- have the same sound pattern as *boat*
- are words from math
- start with *sh*
- have the same spelling pattern as *nice*
- are contractions
- rhyme with *she*

Children are accountable to write their responses and share them with the teacher or the class.

4. Pocket Charts

This center encourages independent language and literacy learning to teach print awareness and comprehension based on short stories, poetry or songs first introduced to the whole class. Ford (1996) used pocket charts to introduce poems and songs at the line and phrase level.

Lines of stories, poetry or songs are selected during whole class instruction by having children point to them after reading them aloud with you.

Make two sentence strips from a selection. Each contains one line of the story, poem or song. Place one of these in the pocket chart. Ask children to read it with you. Then, place the second one in the pocket chart and ask children to read it with you as well. When you finish, remove both strips from the pocket chart and invite one child to replace, organize and match them in the order in which they first appeared. You can do this for the entire selection or use only a passage or verse.

In smaller groups children can work independently or with a partner (PSTT) to examine text more closely, learn to attend to print and develop comprehension as they reorganize lines of text and place them in the pocket chart.

When children have mastered line recognition, cut sentence strips into phrases. Place these phrases in large envelopes and make them available to children working at this center.

Ask them to remove the phrases from an envelope, organize them and match them to a particular sentence from a passage, poem or song. Children are challenged to reassemble lines of a passage, poem or song, phrase by phrase, and match these phrases to the sequenced lines in the pocket chart.

This not only increases children's print awareness but also provides them opportunities to use two sources of information to search, cross-check and problem solve their selections.

After they are proficient at the phrase level cut out the words to a line of the passage, poem or song and place them in an envelope. Ask children to remove the words from the envelope and reassemble the line of text word-by-word.

Ford and Opitz (2002) recommend that you provide children with "blank paper grids" and ask them to copy each word from the selected line. Then, they can cut the "grid" words apart to reconstruct this line or make up another line using their own words.

New lines of short stories, poetry or songs can be introduced regularly and used in these ways to strengthen children's language and literacy acquisition.

5. Short Story, Poem and Song Packs

This center extends work done in Pocket Charts. Children are given large, plastic freezer bags containing phrases or words from a short story, poem or song they organized at the line or phrase level in the Pocket Chart Center. They choose packs according to a specific

The Oracy Instructional Guide
Managing Independent Language and Literacy Learning Centers

level of difficulty, reorganizing and constructing sentences, using phrases or words either to match the originals or create their own innovative versions.

By color-coding phrase or word frames for a particular story, poem or song children are able to easily replace "pieces" in the appropriate freezer bag.

6. Big Books

At this center children have the chance to examine and work with familiar Big Books they have been exposed to through shared reading activities you have modeled.

Known books provide ample opportunities for children to explore text independently and interact with one another, taking turns being the teacher.

To do this, they will need an easel, a pointer, Post-it™ notes, correcting tape and word frames. Working in a small group, they decide who will be the teacher and determine the focus of instruction, i.e., shared reading, word identification, interactive or creative writing.

7. Responding through Art and Puzzles

This center allows children to draw, create an artistic product or reassemble puzzles and *talk* with each other as they work (PSTT). These activities can provide powerful language and learning experiences (Brookes, 1986).

After children have drawn or made something, either independently or as a shared activity, they can *talk* and decide the most important thing they want to say about it. Then, write a caption for their work using invented spellings, spelling scaffolds from the print-rich environment or your support.

If children have constructed a puzzle they can draw a picture of the finished product and add a statement or two to their illustration. Afterward, one child from this center can make a brief presentation of their work to the whole class.

8. Writing

Writing is an excellent adjunct to drawing or creative projects. But it is important for children to write about their experiences and interesting or familiar things and to write letters or messages to friends and loved ones.

Children will need paper, markers, pencils or pens, colorful illustrations, books, toys or other objects in the writing center. For younger children writing is a strong support to language and literacy acquisition. But first they need to *pair, share, think* and *talk* about an experience, object or event about which they want to write.

Talking sets the stage for writing and offers children the chance to explore meanings and clarify their thoughts. Pictures, books and other real things provide children with the scaffolds they need for these purposes. Pairing children at the writing center provides important opportunities for speaking and listening as well as reading, which, like drawing, are natural springboards to early writing.

9. Reading

The reading center should contain a wide assortment of Wordless and multilevel books and magazines. Children can examine or peruse one interesting, new and more difficult book during their time in the reading center but they should be reading extensively. Extensive reading is essential for children to develop language and literacy. They can read independently or with a "buddy." One child reads while the other listens and retells the reader what was read. The reader listens and clarifies or adds to the listener's retelling.

Samway, Whang and Pippit (1995) have created a rich set of additional guidelines to increase the effectiveness of "buddy" reading.

Other language and literacy learning activities in this center can be organized as independent, shared or cooperative work requiring decoding, sight words, vocabulary and comprehension development, or practice reading fluently and dictionary or reference tasks (Morrow, 1996).

10. Computer

A tenth center may be developed using computers. Some children can be taught to use the Internet to strengthen their reading and word processing to write their own stories, poems or songs (Schmar-Doblar, 2003). Websites can be valuable resources to motivate ELL children and those with low language development to read and write: *URL enchantedlearning.com; URL kidspiration.com;* and *URL inspiration.com.*

Independent language and literacy learning centers require low levels of adult monitoring and some freedom with regard to what the children do and how they do it. The children should also be able to work with peers of equal, greater or lesser skill (Weisner, Gallimore and Jordan, 1986).

This frees you to work with Stage I and Stage II children in a small group to provide the kind of intense Oracy instructional interactions necessary for them to learn. The next chapter describes ways to use the components of the OLAI to assist you in this process.

The Oracy Instructional Guide
Managing Independent Language and Literacy Learning Centers

4 Using the Components of the Oral Language Acquisition Inventory (OLAI) to Develop Oracy Instruction

"Children construct meaning through shared activity. Coaching from the environment is needed to create the staggering number of neural connections required for advanced brain development."

L. Vygotsky

The components of the OLAI – Repeated Sentences and Sentence Transformations; Story Reconstruction and Narrative Comprehension; Picture Drawing, Narration and Dictation; and Information Processing and Critical Dialogue – are more than a series of activities for assessment. They create Oracy instructional contexts that link ongoing assessment and teaching interactions.

These assessment and instructional activities can be supplemented with established practices appropriate to a child's stage of language development identified by the results of the OLAI: Read and think-alouds (Wilhelm, 2001), guided, shared and interactive reading and writing (Fountas and Pinnell 1998; 2001; Swartz, Shook and Klein, 1999; Swartz, Klein and Shook, 2001) and independent, extensive reading and writing (Elley and Mangubhai, 1981; 1983; Graves, 1983; Calkins, 1986).

Initially you can follow the same sequence as the OLAI when using the components to organize instruction. Once you are comfortable and proficient in eliciting, restating, expanding and refining language you can change the order to use the activities flexibly and interchangeably.

Component I: Repeated Sentences and Sentence Transformations

Asking children to repeat sentences is one powerful way to measure the level of control they may possess over certain language structures (Clay, et al., 1983).

The emphasis of your interactions during Oracy instruction is on the social uses and functions of language. Repetitions serve to check meanings, fill up a turn and sustain dialogue by acknowledging a new topic or clarifying thoughts, feelings and intentions. This forms a cumulative and collaborative construction of meaning between you and a child (Keenan, 1977).

During the assessment it was suggested you look at children face-to-face. Remain sensitive to the cultural differences of children who are taught not to look at adults when they are talking to them. Making children alter their behavior when they respond to you may be intimidating and can interfere with their responses.

By respecting the child's experiences, listening attentively and responding enthusiastically, you have the opportunity to model the role of an interested learner as well as a teacher.

Besides the social uses developed from repeating sentences this technique supports the development of phonemic awareness, which is the first stage of language development. Knowledge of phonemes is considered by some to be the most important determinant of early success in learning to read and write (Mann, 1991; Stanovich, 1991). But the argument over whether phonological awareness is a precursor or a result of learning to read and write (or both) is still unresolved.

While phonological awareness helps to emphasize the language-related aspects of literacy development and is considered a significant factor (Singer, 1984; Blachman, 1984; Wagner, 1986; Strickland, 1998), "the task of becoming literate cannot be reduced to the learning of a code" (Vernon and Ferreiro, 1999, p. 412). "Overemphasizing phonics may be especially damaging for children who have had few experiences with books prior to school" (Weaver, Gillmeister-Krause and Vento-Zogby, 1996, p. 104).

You use a repeated sentences technique to encourage children to expand and refine their language by rephrasing their responses. This exposes them to different language structures and vocabulary. It helps them reproduce the different structures and terms and identify sounds in words. But the Repeated Sentences assessment protocol is modified for instruction.

Instead of asking children to repeat sentences verbatim as a component of assessment your focus is not on discrepancies between their version and yours or on error. Learning how to "keep the ball in play" is an apt metaphor for what you need to do in order to support children's language acquisition during literacy instruction (Wells, 1986, pp. 47-51).

You do this by finding topics and materials related to shared interests. Incorporate some aspect of what children say, repeating it and extending or refining it. Occasionally invite them to repeat what you say. Use humor in the process when it is appropriate.

Using a repeated sentences model you can incorporate teaching children to hear and identify sounds in words in a powerful, playful and meaningful way.

But working with phonetics or phonemics is just one of the many things young readers and writers need to control.

Durkin, (1995, p.47) said:

This view overlooks children's social intent, their attempts at maintaining dialogue and their awareness of and compensation for their limited resources in conveying meaning. The grammatical view also reduces the function of repetition (and by implication other speech acts) to emulation of the adult model, ignoring any potential communicative purpose. Grammatical competence is presumed to be the child's key goal. As a result, this view assumes that any discrepancy between the child's version and the adult's version is necessarily an error and therefore leads researchers to underestimate children's language abilities and to concentrate on error, not on ability or use.

Using the Components of the Oral Language Acquisition Inventory (OLAI) to Develop Oracy Instruction

Component II: Story Reconstruction and Narrative Comprehension

This component of the OLAI is effective for teaching children to listen, talk about and construct stories and interact with you to interpret narrative and dialogue. Using pictures to listen to a story and retell it develops children's language and comprehension in a meaningful context (Allington, 1995).

Your interaction with children during Story Reconstruction and Narrative Comprehension lays the groundwork for the language development required to read and process story and expository text.

In their exchanges with you, children learn to take risks and use new vocabulary and language structures. They learn strategies that help them problem solve, establish logical order, follow directions and share ideas or feelings. They also learn to make predictions, laugh with you and participate in the joy of discovery. All of these prepare children to participate in school and take part in instructional conversations.

Stories have a sequence: a beginning, a middle and an ending. Children acquiring English as a second language or those whose oral language is not well-developed must learn to follow a story line to interpret a story or "construct" its meaning, not just answer questions about it (Rosenblatt, 1978).

In the current haste to get children with "missed opportunities" reading and writing early, they are led to text before they are led to talk and before they have acquired the language they need to read and construct meaning from commercially published materials. Instead of moving so quickly to published texts they need

Wells (1986, pp. 151-157) said:

Stories teach children the sustained meaning-building organization of written language and its characteristic rhythms and structures. Through listening to stories, children see context built up through the structure of words, not as in oral language, simply through references to immediate surroundings; all the clues from which a child constructs meaning lie in the words. Such meaning building prepares them for the less contextualized language that teachers use and is associated with children's later ability to 'narrate an event', describe a scene and follow instructions. More importantly, it is directly related to children's own inner 'storying,' which they use to create meaning.

opportunities to dictate responses, see their words written down and talk about their own words and experiences. This helps them construct meaning in literacy and learn how text works (Clay, 1993, p.12).

Children must learn to narrate content from pictures and concrete experiences and code observations in their own words before they can make sense of the abstract language found in books (Sulzby, 1985; Hudelson, 1994).

Using the Components of the Oral Language Acquisition Inventory (OLAI) to Develop Oracy Instruction

Component III: Picture Drawing, Narration and Dictation

This component of the OLAI allows children to demonstrate several features of perceptual and psychomotor development that are congruent with learning to read and write. These include the ability to:

• Imagine and create pictures.

• Coordinate hand/eye movements to develop mental imagery, i.e., representative pictures of thoughts, feelings and intentions.

• Use language to define a purpose for drawing.

• Dictate statements about drawings that are written and read.

• Write dictated sentences independently and record sounds in words.

Young children draw before they write to demonstrate more clearly their thoughts and feelings with forms they control until they can use print for this purpose. But drawing is more than a precursor to children's learning to write. It produces a rich synthesis of symbolic processes such as language, mental imagery and creative thought that supports the development of literacy (Bissex, 1980; Brookes, 1986; Dyson, 1986; Gallagher, 1996).

Dictating statements related to the pictures they draw can support children's literacy development because they use their language experiences to direct attention to the early strategies needed to read and write text: learning concepts about print "CAP" (Clay, 2002), learning about print strategies "LAPS" (Reutzel, 1995), hearing and recording sounds in words "HRSIW" (Clay, 1991; 1995) and problem solving unfamiliar words (Elkonin, 1971; Good, Kaminski and Smith, 2001).

The drawing and narration component allows you to establish a relationship of joint attention with children to something in the outside world as you *talk* about their drawings and make a transition from action to speech to clearly communicate.

Shared attention and *talk* are at the core of scaffolding children's language and literacy development and helping them make sense of the way the world works (Bruner, 1983; Wells, 1985).

Smith (1975, p. 47) said:

Prediction through meaningfulness is the basis of language comprehension. By prediction, I do not mean reckless guessing but rather the elimination of unlikely alternatives on the basis of prior knowledge. The child predicts that a limited range of relationships is likely to occur between language and its setting or within the language itself. Meaning then is the relationships the child finds. If there is no meaning to be found, there can be no prediction, no comprehension and no learning. But, to repeat, before meaning can assist a child in learning to read, there must be the insight that print is meaningful.

Using the Components of the Oral Language Acquisition Inventory (OLAI) to Develop Oracy Instruction

Component IV: Information Processing and Critical Dialogue

This component of the OLAI demonstrates children's ability to interact with you and informational text to make: 1) a critical analysis of the content that is objective, using extrapersonal questions; and 2) a personal interpretation or analysis of the content that is more subjective, using intrapersonal questions.

A critical analysis of informational text requires children to uncover facts and identify main ideas to establish the "truth" or logic as presented by an author.

A personal interpretation requires children to use their own knowledge and experiences, thoughts and feelings related to the ideas and information in an academic text.

To be successful in school children must apply a wide range of intrapersonal knowledge to varied extrapersonal reading and writing activities (Tharp and Gallimore, 1988; Gentile and McMillan, 1990; 1995).

Children who struggle with language development can read and write to learn by interacting with teachers and a wide body of literature, expository texts, audiotapes and videos that are significant to them (Veatch and Acinapuro, 1966; Van Allen, 1973; Goldenberg, 1993; Fennessy, 1995; Jewell and Pratt, 1999; Nelson and Linek, 1999; Routman, 1991; 2000).

An instructional approach called Critical Dialogue uses children's background knowledge and experiences to motivate

DuCharme (1992, p.83) said:

Teachers must adopt a broader view of learning to write that encompasses all the symbolic processes. Writing develops in young children as a complex orchestration involving a combination of gesture, speech and drawing. Children must be allowed the opportunity to access the various symbol systems while learning to write.

interest and improve the ability to respond to extrapersonal as well as intrapersonal questions about text (Gentile and McMillan 1992; 1995). More about this approach is discussed in Chapter 8.

Reading and interpreting informational text requires additional skills beyond reading stories (Goodlad, 1984; Goldenberg, 1993). Children have to be able to read and write expository text to participate in content area instructional conversations, write reports and succeed on tests. Learning how to process information for these purposes is the cornerstone of reading and writing to learn in school.

5 Oracy Instruction for Stage I Children

"Every day millions of children arrive at American classrooms in search of more than reading and math skills. They are looking for a light in the darkness of their lives, a Good Samaritan who will stop and bandage a burned heart or ego."

J. Trelease

Children at Stage I in language development can point to illustrations or things in the environment and name or categorize people, animals, objects, places or locations and conditions. They respond using single words or phrases and a few short simple sentences to describe events, activities and experiences.

Examples
Bear, Doggie, House, Sunny, Christmas, etc. These utterances stand in place of more expanded syntax.

Summaries of years of research findings cite three powerful predictors of children's success in literacy learning that occur before coming to school. These are:

- Warm interactions with a caring adult and the *talk* that goes on around pictures and text in storybooks.

- The vocabulary level of the adult reading to the child.

- Identifying some words and letters by visual and auditory discrimination.

Most children who have been read and *talked* to purposefully enter school with the following language and early literacy experiences needed to learn to read and write. They have learned to:

1. Handle books, turn pages, pay attention and focus.

2. Work independently and communicate with an adult to develop language and thinking while taking turns talking and listening.

3. Search for and locate important or interesting things in pictures and then laugh and talk about them.

4. Start a task or problem-solving activity and work through to its completion before moving on to something else.

5. Recognize some words and letters by sound and sight.

6. Connect ideas, answer questions and suggest answers.

7. Ask questions and try something new when learning is confusing or difficult.

8. Follow directions, make choices and participate in a teaching/learning conversation.

9. Confirm or reject responses.

10. Work comfortably and cooperatively with other children.

(Greenspan and Lodish, 1992; Gentile, 1997)

Many children at Stage 1 in language development may not control early literacy learning behaviors. It is the responsibility of the school to provide the opportunities they need to "catch up" to others who may be more experienced (Stevens, 2003).

> *Clay (1997, p. 212) advised:*
>
> *Giving learners opportunities to reveal their range of experience will allow children's personal constructions of meaning to enter into the teaching interaction. Teachers often substitute an environmental explanation for school failure that denigrates the child's home experiences, a view that has come to be known as the deficit model. They talk about the environmentally determined inability as though it were permanent and unalterable, yet they rarely respond to missed opportunities to learn with make-up opportunities.*

Repeated Sentences and Sentence Transformations

Identify children at Stage 1 and focus on them during the read-aloud conversations. Make sure they have opportunities to respond by calling on them and inviting their participation.

This can be difficult because these children are easily intimidated and may remain silent, shrug their shoulders or offer one- or two-word responses. Repeat each utterance, expanding and refining the statement. Occasionally invite the child to repeat it in its modified form.

Children develop a pattern of responding in the classroom in limited ways. The only way to change their habituated practices is to focus on them across the day. Make sure to include them in the instructional conversation, call on them, prompt and scaffold their statements without pressuring them. When you interact in this manner, these children may gradually understand that one- or two-word responses are not acceptable and you expect them to "say more about that."

Read fun rhyming or patterned books, songs or poetry and *talk* about the meanings of words, phrases and ideas. Encourage children to repeat rhymes or structures.

Developing Meaningful Conversations
Directions

1. Make a statement or ask a question.

2. The child responds.

3. Repeat, clarify, expand or refine the child's response.

4. From time to time, ask the child to restate your response and continue the conversation.

Example 1

Teacher: What do you like to do at recess?

Child: Play soccer.

Teacher: So you like to play soccer at recess. Can you say: "I like to play soccer at recess?"

Child: I like to play soccer at recess

Teacher: Good! Why do you like to play soccer at recess?

Child: It's fun!

Teacher: You like to play soccer at recess because it's fun. Now, can you say that? "I like to play soccer at recess because it's fun!"

Child: I like to play soccer at recess because it's fun!

Note: In group work, after one child responds, have the others repeat a statement chorally and then go on to the next child.

Directions

1. The child makes a statement or asks you a question: What? When? Where? How? or Why?

2. You respond by suggesting further inquiry, saying, "That's interesting. What do you think? Let's say more about that."

3. The child responds and you question, confirm, clarify, expand or refine the child's response.

Example 2

Child: Look! I found a feather.

Teacher: That's interesting. It's black. Where did you find it?

Child: On the ground.

Teacher: When did you find it?

Child: Walking to school.

Teacher: So you found a black feather on the ground when you were walking to school.

Child: Uh-huh. (nods)

Teacher: Can you say: "I found a black feather on the ground when I was walking to school."

Child: I found a black feather on the ground when I was walking to school.

A follow-up themed activity might include listening to a story such as *The Fox and the Crow* (Trussell Cullen, 2000. Pearson Education, Inc., publishing as Dominie Press, an imprint of Pearson Learning Group.) and constructing a dialogue. Or have children listen to you read informational text about birds.

Substitute nouns, pronouns and verbs within the structures to change meanings as you talk. For example: I am going to the store. I am going to the bakery. I ran to the store. I ran to the bakery. We are going to the store. We are going to the bakery. We ran to the store. We ran to the bakery.

Story Reconstruction and Narrative Comprehension

Telling stories, reading and talking with Stage 1 children to model language is at the heart of effective Oracy instruction.

Use wordless picture books, illustrations from storybooks or posters to teach children to narrate a logically sequenced story.

- Make sure the children are seated directly in front of you, and speak clearly so they can watch your mouth as you enunciate.

- Model a narration, displaying picture frames as you tell a story. Then ask the children to do the same. Scaffold their effort by providing additional details or information. Use the same book for several days until the children are well-acquainted with the story, its vocabulary and concepts and can provide a fully developed narrative.

- You do not need to exaggerate the volume of your voice or slow down your pronunciation. This can be confusing or disquieting to children.

- When working with ELL children preview, explain and build background knowledge in their first language if you can. Then repeat words and concepts in their second language.

- Encourage the children to use the same words and phrases repetitively in their conversations with you until the words and phrases become a natural part of their expressive language. These interactions facilitate the development of their vocabulary, language structures and communication patterns.

- To expand and refine language say things differently, repeating and rephrasing what you say using short sentences. Through modeling and interactive talk, children learn to listen, experiment with language and acquire new structures and vocabulary. Eventually, they will express themselves more fully. But it takes time.

- When working with ELL children read the same books, stories or informational materials in their first language as well as their second language. Read each book several times. This gives children the opportunity to absorb and think about what you are reading and saying and helps them understand, interpret and make predictions.

- Reinforce the meanings of different words, phrases and concepts by restating them or using pictures, photographs, material objects or other media.

- Pay attention to the children's facial expressions and body language. They will "tell" you when they do not understand or when you are not communicating. They send nonverbal signals in a variety of ways, asking you to repeat, speak slower or say more to clarify meaning.

- In the case of ELL children, use their first language to highlight meaning whenever possible. Incorporate their first language in conversations to foster growth in both languages. Children must first develop the confidence and linguistic competence to be comfortable taking risks with others who have a native command of the second language (Moore, 2001).

To Link Language and Literacy Development:

- Use a story you tell or read to children to elicit a few of their responses and write one or two on a large chart for them to read, discuss and learn something about how text works (Nelson and Linek, 1999).

- Write only those responses that relate to the content. Structure the reading and discussion to include literacy learning skills and problem solving strategies, i.e., CAP, LAPS or HRSIW, so they are directly connected to the children's *talk* written down.

- Participate with the children in enrichment activities and talk with them while playing games, writing songs and poetry, dancing or role-playing.

- Ask the children to listen and respond for specific purposes as they are read to or after they have listened to segments of audiotapes or watched portions of videos.

- Use a variety of visual materials to teach vocabulary and concept development and to help the children develop control over the most common sentence structures.

Story reconstruction and narrative comprehension activities provide you opportunities to expand and refine children's language production as you listen to their narration and prompt them to insert more or varied vocabulary and concepts.

Phonemic Awareness

Infuse explicit phonemic awareness activities as an integral part of language and literacy development at all levels.

Phonemic or phonological awareness is the ability to hear and manipulate distinct sounds in spoken language. It requires hearing sounds in words, identifying where the sounds change and being able to segment the sounds when they break. This is complex in English when compared to Spanish and many other languages, and it requires planned, direct instruction in meaningful contexts.

With only a few exceptions each sound in Spanish corresponds one-to-one with each letter and in most cases, syllables have one vowel and are clearly separated (*ma-ri-po-sa*,

compared to *pop-py*). Some exceptions are in words like *cuesta (cues-ta)*, *cueva (cue-va)*, *puente (puen-te)*, *puerta (puer-ta)* and *cielo (cie-lo)*.

Activities may include identifying and practicing:
- Syllabication by clapping and counting syllables. Identifying "chunks" in words helps children to develop rapid and efficient decoding as opposed to letter-by-letter analysis of unfamiliar words.

- Onset (one or more consonants appearing before the first vowel at the beginning of a word) and rime (the ending or last part of a word: *b-ug, pl-ug, shr-ug*). Determining when words are alike or different at the beginning and end is a significant step toward learning how to "sound out" unfamiliar words.

- Beginning and ending sounds in spoken words. For example, *cat* and *cap* and *shop* and *shake* begin with the same sounds but end with different sounds, while *top* and *hop* and *tops* and *hops* begin with different sounds but end with the same sounds.

- Blending and segmenting sounds at the beginning, in the middle or at the end of words: *bl, cr, squ, cl, dr, fl, spl*, etc.; *oa, ie, ow, ou, ai, ei*, etc.; and *sh, ch, th, ng*, etc.

- Dropping sounds and pronouncing the remaining sounds. For example, *(bl)and, pa(tch), (fl)ash*.

- Swapping sounds. For example, *(sm)ack/(bl)ack* or *(fl)it/(qu)it*.

- Rhyming words: *car* and *star*, *tack* and *black*, etc.

- Sequencing magnetic letters to construct children's names, names of family members or friends and high frequency or favorite words.

The Diamond and Four

Using a modification of Brunn's, (2002, p. 523) four square strategy, you can target those phonemic elements that children need to identify using only minimal time each week. Children keep a Diamond and Four booklet containing the following diagram and target phonetic elements, words, and sentences for each day. Preschool/kindergarten children can copy the phonemic element in the diamond and name words they know that begin with it.

Example

The Diamond and Four
Targeted Phonemic Element

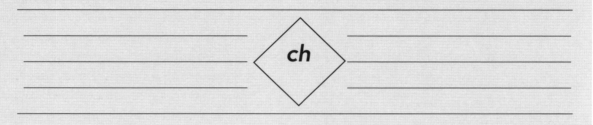

Brunn explains that the consonant cluster *ch* appears in the middle of the four-square diagram for each of five lessons for one week. The cluster remains the same across time but changes occur to illustrate this phonemic element as an onset (first "chunk" in a word) or rime (last "chunk"). On the last two lines, children can write a sentence using as many of the words containing the targeted phoneme as they can.

Monday:	*chicken, church, Charlie, chin*	Thursday:	*witch, ditch, charm, chant*
Tuesday:	*catch, which, watch, match*	Friday:	*chase, choose, chalk, change*
Wednesday:	*cherry, cheese, chart, chirp*		

These words are grouped by association to support children's ability to construct sentences. As an example, Brunn suggests: "Charlie's chin dripped with chicken at the church dinner."

Picture Drawing, Narration and Dictation

Example: Shared Drawing

Allow the children to work in pairs when doing shared drawing (PSTT). Instruct them to share the marker, taking turns, to "draw something beautiful." They will have to talk to each other to determine who goes first, what the other person has in mind and how to proceed. Each child makes a mark on the paper, and then the other child adds to the mark. They should talk to each other as they continue to draw.

When they have finished ask them to decide what they would like to say about the drawing.

Then write their statement above or below the illustration. Support their efforts to write these statements. They can also help each other with spelling, sequence and structure. Then ask them to take turns reading what they have written.

Stage I children learn to write by drawing a "global" picture of an idea. Next, they move on to scribbles or balls and lines, which may resemble cursive or print. Then they progress to single letters that represent whole words (Clay, 1975; Durkin, 1995, p.405).

Provide children an opportunity to draw using explicit instruction (Brookes, 1986). This approach develops children's: 1) ear/hand/eye coordination; 2) visual perception; 3) visual discrimination; 4) spatial organization; 5) specific vocabulary for academic, content learning; and 6) the ability to listen and follow directions to draw a recognizable person, animal or object.

In addition to learning to draw children learn to follow simple directions that require mind/body connections. This can be done as a group activity or as part of a game. For example: "Jump up and down," "Point at your nose," "Turn the pages," "Take out your pencils or markers," "Turn your books upside down," "Draw a line under _____" or "Circle _____."

Information Processing and Critical Dialogue

Use the interactive format from Component IV of The *Oral Language Acquisition Inventory*. Read short segments of informational text and *talk* with the children about the topic, i.e., people, animals, insects, trees, plants, planets or different cultures.

Listen to segments of audiotapes containing supplemental information or watch portions of videos focused on biology, sociology, geography, botany or zoology. This can expand the dialogue and motivate children to acquire content vocabulary and concepts.

6 Oracy Instruction for Stage II Children

"Language is the naming of experience, and what we name we have power over."

J. Kingman

Continue using Oracy instructional activities from Stage I, but select more challenging content to prepare the children for reading and writing expository text.

Children at Stage II in language development can formulate phrases and longer, simple sentences containing prepositional phrases.

These sentences typically employ the verb *to be* coupled with action words containing *-ing* to talk about pictures, i.e., people, animals, objects, places or locations and to describe conditions, events, activities and experiences.

Children at Stage II primarily use the present tense and common vocabulary terms. They can ask What, When, Where and Why questions and transform statements into simple negatives, questions, imperatives or exclamations.

Examples
"My mom is nice." "He is going home." "Those are my toys!" "It's raining." "I like ice cream." "When can I go?" "Where are my shoes?" "Minnie has no hat." "Hey, don't do that!" "I love my puppy!"

Repeated Sentences and Sentence Transformations

Once children control phrases and some simple sentences, they are able to play the human sentence expansion and refinement game. This is a good way to start each day because it focuses the children and involves the whole class.

Each day you select a topic by asking the children what they would like to talk about. This might be chosen from a variety of topics, including plants, persons, minerals, vehicles, games, toys or animals.

For example, in Mrs. Ricka Pirani's, first-grade classroom (Robert Randall Elementary School, Milpitas, California), the children decided to talk about a wolf. This was the subject of a story that was read to them the day before. The teacher said, "Who wants to be the wolf?" The child who volunteered became the first link in the human sentence and took a position standing in front of the class. Afterward children volunteered one at a time to represent the remainder of an expanded sentence. They lined up next to each other to become each part after the teacher prompted for the expansion by asking, "Who?" "What?" "Where?" "When?" "How?" or "Why?"

The teacher stood right behind each child, placing a hand over the child's head and reciting each part while the children repeated what she said until the completed sentence was formed. "The wolf" "was running and jumping" "in the woods" "because he was happy."

As each new child joined the line, the teacher held her hand over that child's head and the other children repeated that portion of the sentence in unison. This gave the children multiple opportunities to practice patterning language, which is critical to acquiring control over these structures.

By changing children's positions in the human sentence, you create a more challenging listening and responding activity. When children are reorganized in the sentence, they cannot just memorize their contribution but must attend to, store and retrieve the full utterance.

There are many possibilities for expanding and refining children's oral language and raising the level of their vocabulary and comprehension, using the human sentence technique.

Scaffolding children's responses by expanding the structures and refining vocabulary using a more colorful or precise term is a powerful way to add new language and concepts.

Asking children to transform the sentence into a negative, question, command or exclamation supports learning how to control the sound structures of language. Afterwards, write the "human sentence" on a white board and invite children to read it along with you.

Developing Dictation Charts

There are two approaches to developing dictation charts. Both should be used because they provide different experiences for children to develop language and literacy. One requires children to listen while being read to or told a story and then respond. The other requires children to actually observe, make something or do something and respond.

For listening and responding use a variety of materials such as stories, poetry, songs, informational texts and audiotapes. For observing, doing things or making things, use illustrations, objects, drawings, audiotapes, videos and various creative activities related to content area learning.

After reading to the children or engaging them in an activity open a conversation. One way to start is by asking them to tell the most important thing they learned. Write some of their responses in large bold print on chart paper displayed on an easel or taped to the chalkboard and talk about each one (Van Allen, 1968; Stauffer, 1980; Bernstein, 1981; Ogle, 1986; Combs, 1987; Nelson and Linek, 1999). Extend children's responses from time to time (expansion), or use a different word in place of one the children may have used (refinement).

As you write the words, ask the children to help you spell a few of them. This helps children focus, follow the sequence of sounds and letters left to right across a word, listen to the sounds and identify corresponding written letters.

In the following two sections—*Reading to Children* and *Combining a Hands-on Activity with Literacy Learning*—two examples for developing dictation charts are provided. The first is a dialogue based on an informational text the teacher reads to the children. The second combines reading with an activity, in this case *planting seeds*. Both dialogues and charts are drawn from Mrs. Jeanine Alvarado's class at Heritage School in Lodi, California.

Reading to Children

Dialogue — Example 1

<u>Spiders</u>

Teacher: What's the most important thing you learned about spiders?

Child: They lay eggs.

Teacher: Yes they do. They lay eggs in a sac.

Child: Some eat bees.

Teacher: Some eat bees and other insects.

Child: Spiders make webs to catch insects.

Teacher: Yes, they trap them. Spiders make webs to trap insects.

Dictation Chart — Example 1

<u>Spiders</u>

Page 1
Spiders have eggs. They lay their eggs in an egg sac. Some spiders have red spots. They have eight legs. They have eight eyes, too. A spider has a mouth and fangs.

Page 2
Spiders have hair and claws on their feet. Spiders shed their skin. Some spiders can swim. Some eat bees and other insects. Sometimes they eat each other.

Page 3
Spiders make webs to trap insects. When a fly gets stuck, they wrap it up. They poison it and eat it by sucking it. Black widow spiders kill and eat their husbands.

After the dictation and recording on the chart, tell the children you will read each page to them. But first ask:
• Where do I start reading?
• Which way do I go?
• Then where do I go?
• Where do I stop reading?
• What is the first word on this page?
• What is the first letter in the word spider?
• What is the last letter in spider?
• These interactions provide an opportunity to teach CAP.

Then use a pointer while you read out loud, pointing to each word on the chart. Ask the children to follow the pointer with their eyes. When you finish, invite them to read as you point and match, one-to-one.

You can mask structure and content words or parts of these words (onsets or rimes) on the chart pages using Post-it notes. When the masked word appears in the text, ask the children to make predictions and identify the word based on first/last letter or "chunk," syntax, etc. Then ask them, "How did you know that word was _____?"

This provides an opportunity to teach CAP, LAPS and HRSIW.

You can also teach lower text processing strategies, i.e., moving left-to-right and top-to-bottom, self-monitoring by pointing and matching one-to-one and identifying familiar or unfamiliar words in context.

Finally, invite one child to read the first page

"just like I did," pointing to the written words and reading them aloud. Another child reads the second page and another reads the last page. Ask the other children to follow the pointer or the child's pointing finger and follow along silently.

Combining a Hands-on Activity with Literacy Learning

This requires children to do something and talk, read and write about it. In the following example the teacher explains to the children that they will be planting seeds and watching every day for the seeds to sprout. They are told to listen to an informational text about seeds and how to plant them and then talk about and write how it will be done before they begin planting.

Dialogue — Example 2

Seeds

Teacher: Class, what are we going to do today?

Child #1: We're planting seeds.

Teacher: Yes, we are planting seeds in a pot of dirt.

Child #1: We are planting seeds in a pot of dirt.

Teacher: Then what do we do?

Child #2: We will make a hole in the dirt.

Teacher: We will make a hole in the dirt and bury the seeds. Now, let's say that together.

Everyone: We will make a hole in the dirt and bury the seeds.

Teacher: Good! Now, what do the seeds need to grow?

Child #3: They need sun and water to grow.

Teacher: Yes, the seeds need sunshine and water so they can sprout.

Child #3: They need sunshine and water so they can sprout.

Teacher: What happens next?

Child #4: They grow more.

Teacher: Yes, next the plants grow taller and taller.

Child #4: Next, the plants grow taller and taller.

Teacher: Then what happens?

Children: They grow little flowers and turn into beans.

Teacher: Yes! Finally, they bloom and produce beans. Let's say that together.

Everyone: Finally, they bloom and produce beans.

The children's responses to the teacher form the text of the dictation chart. The teacher expands and refines some of the responses as they are dictated and asks individual children, or the group, to repeat expansions or refinements before recording them. The teacher makes sure every child participates.

Dictation Chart — Example 2
Seeds

Page 1
We're planting seeds *in a pot of dirt*. We will make a hole in the dirt *and bury the seeds*. The seeds need *sunshine and water so they can sprout*.

Page 2
Next, the plants grow taller and taller. Finally, they bloom and produce beans.

The second example can be a journal writing activity as well as a dictation and reading exercise. Ask the children to draw a picture about planting seeds. Then have them write the steps and directions for planting and growing seeds, using the charts as references when necessary. Encourage them to do as much as they can independently or by working with a partner.

Independent Writing

At the conclusion of the dictation and reading the children can write independently in their journals.

Leave the dictation chart pages on display so they can use them to reference spellings of words and language structures. The children can write their favorite statement(s) from one of the chart pages or add new ones. Allow them to work individually or in pairs so they can edit each other's writing and provide support when necessary.

Circulate while the children are writing, helping them expand and refine their individual responses. Later, add one or two of the children's independent statements to those recorded on the dictation charts.

Guided and Shared Writing and Reading

Shared writing as well as independent writing helps children clarify the use of common language structures and vocabulary (Graves, 1983; Calkins, 1986).

You can combine some of the written statements from the dictation charts and one or

two of those written independently to create computer-generated booklets. These booklets support children's reading for meaning, learning lower and higher text-processing strategies and problem-solving skills because they are drawn from texts the children constructed. Make one for each child and use these booklets for guided, shared or independent reading.

During guided reading, elicit and build background knowledge and set purposes for the children's reading before they read, during the reading and after the reading is completed.

Use the booklets to take a Running Record of one child's reading each day. (For a full explanation of administering and interpreting Running Records see Clay, 1993.)

Do shared reading using Big Books (Holdaway, 1981; Bedrova and Leong, 1996) and teach CAP, LAPS and HRSIW in the same way you did with the dictation charts.

Teach the higher level processing strategies through interactions with the children and the big books, i.e., self-monitoring, searching for cues (meaning, structure, phonemic and visual information), cross-checking and self-correction.

Booklets can also be developed to do shared, interactive writing and editing as children record statements elicited from their drawings, conversations or experiences (Keene and Zimmerman, 1997; Swartz, Klein and Shook, 2001).

This provides opportunities for you to prompt children in ways that support their expanded and refined statements, enhance phonemic awareness and explicitly model fluent reading and writing. It also supports the children in their effort to write high frequency and favorite words and complete sentences.

Providing children with shared instruction that combines language development and writing is an effective way to support their acquisition of common language structures and the ability to write expository text. For example, in one teacher's classroom the children were asked to decide on and write about an event. The children talked among themselves about a recent situation. Two men were called to come to the school and remove a ball wall that had collapsed. (Patricia Curry's classroom, Kawana Elementary School, Santa Rosa, California).

Event: Toby and B.J. were called to haul away a ball wall that had fallen.

Where did it happen? Kawana Elementary School.

Who was there? Some of the teachers, children, B.J. and Toby.

What happened? "One day B.J. and Toby came to Kawana School because the ball wall fell over."

Text: "First, B.J. got out of his truck. Next, he tied the rope around the ball wall. Then, he pulled the ball wall out and took it to the garbage can. Finally, he went away and came back with a new ball wall."

This shared writing activity was developed as the teacher talked with the children and while the children talked with each other to describe this event. The teacher was able to help shape some of their responses so they contain several of the most common structures featuring prepositional phrases and conjunctions. The approach lends itself to supporting and clarifying children's language production and allows you to interact with them to expand and refine responses before recording them on chart paper.

Word Walls

Create a word wall containing 100-125 or more of the most common or high frequency words. Print these words in bold black letters. Cut them out, laminate them and pin or tape them in alphabetical order to the wall, bulletin board or poster board at the children's eye level. Teach the children how to reference these high frequency words on the word wall so they can spell them accurately during writing activities (Allington and Cunningham, 1998).

There are commercial word frames that can be removed from their backing on the wall and replaced. Children can take these to their seats and return them to the wall when they are finished using them as referents for their writing.

Fluency

You can help children in Stages I and II become fluent readers by practicing reading portions of the dictation charts and big books to develop comprehension and fluency using Line-by-Line

The following is a partial list of other time connectors:	
After that	*A long time ago*
Immediately	*Long after that*
One (second/minute/ hour/day/year)	*Meanwhile*
Soon after that	*At the same time*
The next day	*That (morning/afternoon /evening)*
Later on	
In the beginning	*Today*
In the end	*Yesterday*
At (give time)	*Tomorrow*

Protocol (Langer, Bartolome, Vasquez and Lucas, 1990).

This protocol is particularly helpful for children struggling with oral language development as well as those acquiring a second language. It focuses on repeated reading and develops a child's control of language structure, understanding of vocabulary and concepts and fluency, i.e., phrasing, smoothness and pace.

The protocol is a powerful teaching procedure that can be used individually or with small or large groups.

Passages of text are presented one line at a time, and the children are asked to interpret, make predictions and talk about concepts or provide the meanings of specific words before they read.

The approach requires children to build on comprehension and fluency to read each line and the following line in a smooth cadence. Read the first line and ask children to, "Read it like this." Then the children read the first line.

When children can read this line fluently, go to the second line and read it. When they read this line fluently, return to the beginning, reading the first and second lines fluently in sequence before moving to the next line.

Each time a new line is mastered, children return to the beginning and read all the lines to that point, until the passage is read as a whole. If children read a line haltingly or word by word, model fluency by rereading that line and the next one. The protocol has three advantages for teaching fluency:

1. As children work to develop vocabulary and concepts related to the passage, they clarify meanings and add new information. This scaffolds deeper comprehension as they practice reading the lines, *talking* with you about them and then rereading.

2. It "chunks" text and teaches children to invoke strategies used by able readers to self-monitor during reading, i.e., reread at the point of difficulty or error and search for cues, cross-check using two sources of information and self-correct to construct meaning.

3. It scaffolds children's efforts through teacher modeling and patterned, repetitive readings to correct misunderstanding, pronounce words correctly and develop fluency.

Oracy Instruction/Small Groups: Talk/Before-During-After — Stages I-II

- Follow a theme.
- Integrate Listening, Speaking, Reading, Writing, Viewing. Restate children's responses, expand and refine language.
  - Hands-on Activity: Draw, make or do something centered on the theme. *Talk/before, during-after.*
  - Read alouds-think alouds: *Talk/before-during-after.*
  - Picture frames and story narration: *Talk/before-during-after.*
- Develop a dictation chart.
  - Shared writing: *Talk/before-during-after.*
- Use the chart for shared reading. Focus on concepts about print, phonemic analysis, word and letter formation, high frequency words, important, difficult, interesting or colorful words.
- Interactive writing: Children collaborate (*pair, share, think and talk*) to write an additional statement.
- Combine the chart with written statements to develop shared or guided reading "texts." Children illustrate pages of these "books."

7 Oracy Instruction for Stages III and IV Children

"Even if you're on the right track, if you just sit there, sooner or later a train will come along and run you over."

Will Rogers

Continue using Oracy instructional activities from Levels I and II and add a wider array of literature and writing activities.

Children at Stages III and IV in language development can produce connected discourse using multiple prepositions and conjunctions (Monroe, 1965).

They begin to use the past and future tenses. They also use more flexible and advanced vocabulary to talk about people, animals, objects, places and locations in illustrations and to describe activities, events, conditions and experiences.

Stage III and IV children may use pronouns more accurately and they can establish cause-effect relationships. They typically use multiple prepositions and conjunctions in their responses. They control more extensive vocabulary and can use not only the present and past tenses but the future as well.

Examples
"He likes apples *and* bananas."
"She smiles *because* she's happy."
"My mom *was* out in the kitchen."
"He *went* home because it got dark."
"It is raining on my head *and* I am all wet."
"I *like* ice cream with my dessert."
"Minnie has no hat *because* she lost it."

They ask complex questions and transform more complex statements as negatives, questions, commands and exclamations.

Examples
"Can I go play at the park if I finish my homework?"
"Don't do that to my cat or I'll tell."
"I love my puppy so she can sleep in my bed."

Vocabulary and Concept Development

Continue using activities from Stages I and II and incorporate commercially published "little books" and expository texts for shared and guided reading and writing that focus on the children's experiences and interests. Books should feature the structures, vocabulary and concepts children use in their oral language but may contain some language that is slightly beyond their control (Vygotsky, 1962; Luria, 1976).

Use an adaptation of the four-square strategy (Brunn, 2002), The Diamond and Four, to teach content vocabulary and concepts. Children can develop a vocabulary/concept booklet like the targeted phonemic element booklet described previously in Stage I Oracy instruction. Each day you and the children select and *talk* about an important event, concept, difficult or colorful word.

Draw the Diamond and Four diagram on large chart paper and write the targeted word in the middle of the diamond. Ask the children to provide other words they know that are related to this concept. Then ask them to recreate the diagram and write the targeted word/concept and four related words on a single page of the vocabulary/concept booklet.

For preschool and kindergarten children you should duplicate in advance the Diamond and Four design on the pages of their booklets. They can copy or write the targeted word in the diamond.

The Diamond and Four

Example

The Diamond and Four
Targeted concept = a pack

Monday: *pack/* A *pack* of wolves is like a family and hunts in a gang.

Tuesday: *evil/* Some people think wolves are *evil.* (bad, harmful, wicked, savage)

Wednesday: *fierce/* Wolves *are fierce* when they fight for food. (cruel, ferocious, violent, intense)

Thursday: *howl/* Wolves *howl* at night before they go out hunting. (bawl, wail, cry, moan)

Friday: *nuzzle/* All the wolves *nuzzle* the leader to show they will obey. (rub, snuggle, press, cuddle)

Choosing Texts

Matching texts to children's level of language development and control provides the linguistic scaffolds they need to read independently and construct meaning. Begin shared, guided and independent reading of these books teaching CAP, LAPS, HRSIW and basic and higher strategies so children learn how to problem solve unfamiliar words, comprehend and read fluently (Fountas and Pinnell, 1996).

Engage children in meaningful conversations about these texts and talk about new or different vocabulary and concepts. Read and talk about academic or content area vocabulary and concepts (Chamot and O'Malley, 1989; Cummins, 1995).

Read more expository or informational books to the children and talk with them about phenomena in their social (experiential) and physical (environmental) worlds to develop vocabulary, comprehension and fluency.

Early Writing to Support Language and Literacy Development

Encourage children to write letters to you, their parents, relatives or friends and to one another. These letters can contain messages or a note of thanks or appreciation (see examples at right).

Children can write letters to characters from stories they read or books that have been read to them. They can draw names from a bag and

Letter Writing—Example 1

February 9, 2003

Dear Ms. Montgomery,

Today we will bake a gingerbread boy. Everyone likes to bake cookies. Can we eat him tomorrow?

Love,

Marci

Letter Writing—Example 2

February 12, 2003:

Dear Ms. Stapleton,

Thank you for coming to our class and talking to us about your dog. We learned a lot about feeding and taking care of pets. It was fun listening to you! Will you come back again?

Sincerely,

Mrs. Montgomery's Class

write a letter to a pen pal or create a weekly response journal in which they write a letter to a family member each week to tell them what went on in school. They can write about field trips or excursions. Afterwards, the children can read these letters to each other or to the class (LeVine, 2002).

Story Reconstruction and Narrative Comprehension

Tell stories and draw pictures, then discuss them and write about them. Continue teaching children to narrate stories using wordless books but now include an accompanying script. They should be able to listen as you read the script, looking at each picture from start to finish, and then retell the story while looking back at the pictures. Show portions of stories on videotapes and ask the children to describe the characters, the sequence of events or the settings. Use information videos related to plant and animal life, space, different cultures, historical figures or events, geography, music, art, math or science and conduct critical dialogues around these topics (see pages 38–41).

Prompt children to expand and refine language in ways that make their storytelling and interpretations more interesting or colorful.

Example

You said, "The shoes are hanging on the line. Some guys threw them." How can you say that and make it more interesting?

(The shoes are dangling on the line because some guys flung them up there.)

Guided and Shared Writing and Reading

ELL children and those struggling to acquire language and literacy do not gain much from whole class instruction, even from explicit modeling, verbal explanations or from skills, conventions and spelling instruction (McNaughton, 1995; Glasswell, Parr and McNaughton, 2003). They lack the necessary language development to understand instruction or directions voiced from a distance so are unable to meet teachers' goals and expectations. They require more intense, personal interactions with you and a few other children before they can benefit from working in a large group (Stanovich, 1986; Cazden, 1988). Themed activities scaffold vocabulary development and comprehension.

Glasswell, Parr, and McNaughton (2003, p. 496) said:

We see development and learning on the one hand and teacher guidance on the other as taking place within activities occurring in a classroom. From the perspective of the child, these can be (a) joint activities with a teacher or peers, (b) personal activities done in relative independence of other class members yet structured by the teacher.

Conducting a Shared Reading and Writing Activity

Materials for the Teacher
Easel

Big Book; *Brown Bear, Brown Bear*

Chart paper

Sheets of blank paper divided in half so children have a practice page and a writing page

Black markers

Magnetic letters

ABC chart on the wall and a Word Wall containing approximately 100-125 of the most frequently appearing words in text

A separate sheet of notebook paper to record your observations

Materials for the Children
Multicolored nontoxic markers

Dry or erasable markers and small erasers

Individual white boards and individual size ABC charts

Objectives
To develop children's:
- concepts about print and looking at print strategies
- ability to identify high frequency words
- phonemic awareness
- letter and word knowledge

Procedures
Dictated responses or stories make ideal material to conduct shared reading and writing activities. Introduce the big book *Brown Bear, Brown Bear*. Display the cover and talk about it with the children. Then read each page containing the structure, "Brown Bear, Brown

Bear what do you see?" Next, point to an adjoining page and placing the pointer under each word read, "I see a _____ looking at me."

As you turn the pages, talk about the animals in the story. Encourage the children to read along with you. Continue doing this and talk about each page with the children until the story is finished.

After the shared reading of the story *Brown Bear, Brown Bear* close the book and put it to one side. On a sheet of the chart paper write a title for the story you will write with the children. For example, *We See Some Animals Looking At Us*. Survey the group asking them to identify all the animals they see in the story. After the children have made several responses, ask one child, "What do you see?" The child responds, "I see a red bird looking at me."

Ask all the children to repeat this sentence as you write it on the chart. Having children orally rehearse these sentences will strengthen their ability to make predictions and establish control of the language structure, "I see a _____ looking at me."

Learning Concepts About Print regarding first and last and distinguishing between a letter and word are important textual markers for children. Point to the first sentence, "I see a red bird looking at me." Ask the children, "What is the first word in our story?" If they struggle with this, point to the word *I* and say: "*I* is the first word. Now, what is the last word?" If they are unsure, point to the word *me* and say: "*Me* is the last word."

Now ask one of the children to come forward and point to the first and last words in the story. Do the same to establish the concept of a letter and a word. Point to the word *me*. Say:

"Now, let's look at the word *me*. Let's count the letters in *me*." Point to each letter and identify them by letter name. "There are two letters in this word, *m* and *e*. Let's count the number of words in our story so far." Point to each word as you count. Then say: "There are eight words." Ask one child to come forward and, using the pointer, count the number of words. The other children repeat by counting in unison.

Afterward, ask another child to add a response to the story. Say: "What do you see?" The child says: "I see a white dog looking at me." Repeat this statement, encouraging the children to do so as well. Ask the children, "What is the first word in this part of our story?" Say "I" as you point to it and frame it with your two index fingers. Point out the space between the words *I* and *see*. The children say: "I." Now say: "Yes, I see a white dog looking at me." Show the children the spaces between the rest of the words on the page.

Now ask them to write *I* or *me* on their whiteboards. This provides an opportunity for them to practice writing a known word.

Directionality is taught during interactive writing as well. Move to the chart and ask: "Where do I start writing?" Point to the upper left side of the page as you write the word *I*. Ask the children to point to the upper left side of the whiteboard at their desks. Say: "Point to where you will write the word *I*." Then ask: "Which way do I go after I write the word *I*?" Demonstrate with your back to the children the proper left-to-right movement across the chart as you finish writing, "I see a white dog looking at me." Ask again, "After I write the word *I*, which way do I go?" Demonstrate with the pointer the left-to-right direction and ask the children to use their

finger to move left-to-right across the whiteboard just as you did with the pointer.

Now ask one child to come up and write the word *I* on a blank sheet of paper displayed on the easel. Then ask the other children to write the word *I* in the left-hand corner of their whiteboards. They may need to refer to their ABC chart or a magnetic letter to do this. Then have them erase these trials.

It is clear that learning to hear and record sounds in words is an important step in early reading and writing success. Children can practice slowly saying a word, listening for the component sounds and writing one or more of the corresponding letters. For example, "I'm going to say the word *me*. Listen carefully." Prolong the sounds of *m* and *e* as you say the word. Now ask the children to do the same, ("*mmm—eee*").

Then ask the children, "Which sounds do you hear? Do you hear the /m/? Do you hear the /ē/? Let's do it again, slowly." Finally, ask the children to write the first sound in the word *me* on their whiteboards. They may have to refer to their ABC charts to form the letters. Do the same with the letter *e*.

You can practice writing other high frequency words (*we, see, some, a, at, us*, etc.) and hearing and recording sounds in these words as well.

Children can practice clapping words that have more than one syllable to hear and identify component parts of words. For example, say: "Listen and watch. I'm going to clap the parts of the word *looking*." Say and clap both parts of *look—ing*. Invite the children to join you in saying and clapping *look—ing*. Afterward, ask: "How many parts are there in *look—ing*?"

After the children practice hearing and recording sounds in words and listening and clapping a multi-syllabic word, they can attempt writing several of the high frequency words in this story on the whiteboards. They may need to cross-check their spelling using the dictation or ABC charts, magnetic letters or Word Wall words. Ask them to write one whole sentence on the whiteboards. They can work individually or in pairs, talking to each other and sharing the pen.

Finally, they can co-write the story using the references mentioned above. The result might look something like this.

We See Some Animals Looking At Us

I see a red bird looking at me.

I see a white dog looking at me.

The End

Stages III and IV children benefit from writing as a shared or joint activity. They can learn to write a multitude of letters and words and compose stories with a logical beginning, middle and ending by sharing the pen with the teacher as well as with each other.

These children also benefit from a structure or external scaffolding for learning to write expanded informational text that explains how to do something or addresses a topic containing a main idea and related details.

This is appropriate for these children because they can use their control over more expanded and refined language skills to develop vocabulary, comprehension and fluency. Their strengths provide necessary scaffolds for them to self-monitor and solve problems as they read and write for meaning (Monroe, 1965; Clay, 1995).

Example

How to Make a Peanut Butter Sandwich

First: We need a knife, some bread and a jar of peanut butter.

Next: Put two pieces of bread on the table, side by side.

Then: Open the jar. Stick the knife into the peanut butter and scoop some out.

Last: Spread the peanut butter on one piece of bread. Put the two pieces together.

That's how to make a peanut butter sandwich.

---

8 Oracy Instruction for Stage V Children

"Self is the sole subject we study and learn. I bring myself to sea, to Malta, to Italy, to find new affinities between myself and my fellow men, to observe narrowly the affections, weaknesses, surprises, hopes, doubts, which new sides of panorama shall call forth in me."

Ralph Waldo Emerson

Continue using Oracy instructional activities from Stages I-IV to connect language and literacy.

Children at Stage V formulate complete sentences and control multiple prepositions and conjunctions as well as relative pronouns and adverbial clauses. They also control inflected endings.

Examples

"My mama is the one who will get it for me."

"It rains on my head whenever I walk outside."

"Put my hat in her box, otherwise she might get hurt."

"Actually, Minnie lost her hat when she fell off the swing."

They can benefit from more complex guided, interactive and independent reading and writing activities. These children are also flexible in the way they express themselves and can begin or end a response with a "moveable" expansion or connecting word or clause. For example:

"It was late when I got home." "When I got home it was late."

"We can go if you'll let us." "If you'll let us we can go."

"They are building houses where we used to play." "Where we used to play they are building houses."

Stage V children demonstrate control of the most common sentence structures and sentence transformations. Once children reach this stage of language competence they can benefit from more varied conversation, reading and writing challenges.

Now, they need to sharpen the ability to analyze, reason and express opinions and feelings. Then they can draw inferences and make clear summaries, not just provide details. They should be able to identify themes and motives, pose questions and make predictions. This allows them to make connections between what they read or write and what they have learned, i.e., to apply what is read, not just retell it. They have to learn to respond to differentiated inquiry and make interpretations.

Two instructional approaches provide Stage V children more challenging opportunities to strengthen their language and literacy: 1) Cloze Procedure (Taylor, 1953), and 2) Critical Dialogues (Gentile and McMillan, 1995).

1. Cloze Procedure requires children to read a narrative or expository passage that contains an intact first and last sentence and several related sentences. These sentences contain a blank space for every fifth word up to the last sentence. Children read the entire passage first and then work in pairs (PSTT) to fill in the blank spaces with words that make sense. Cloze passages can strengthen children's writing and use of language structures as well as content vocabulary and comprehension.

2. Critical Dialogues can enhance children's inferential thinking, ability to distinguish fact from fiction, pose questions, make interpretations, predictions and applications and develop the language of emotion. These dialogues help prepare children to participate in academic conversations and perform successfully in regular classrooms.

Critical Dialogues

A critical dialogue is a structured conversation that engages children in talking about story and information, posing problems and ethical dilemmas that link their personal experiences to content. Their life experiences can be used as a basis for dialogue and are assets for teaching that may otherwise go unnoticed (Pogrow, 1988; Moll, 1990; Gentile and McMillan, 1992; 1995).

Freire (1985) used dialogues to develop Brazilian peasants' literacy using their personal experiences and situations to help them connect language, thought and reality.

Critical dialogue instruction is developed using a triangular curriculum: excerpts from quality literature, related expository passages and portions of audiotapes or videos.

Dialogues incorporate reading, writing and creative activities. Language and literacy learning are extended through the use of videos related to content subjects, i.e., geography, geology, ecology, biology, zoology, botany, sociology, history, art and music.

A great deal of language development and literacy learning can occur using small amounts of text. These excerpts are important because you can build motivation by supplementing or changing the material and activities almost daily.

While some children may struggle to learn because of their language limitations, many have a store of intrapersonal knowledge and life experiences related to polarized themes of the human condition. This helps them find meaning in language and literacy activities and helps stimulate conversation.

Some of these themes are: life and death; good and evil; love and indifference; kindness and malevolence; joy and sorrow; perseverance and surrender; confrontation and compromise; purpose and aimlessness; belonging and alienation; honor and dishonor; hope and despair; vitality and lethargy; loyalty and treachery; courage and cowardice; generosity and greed; forthrightness and dishonesty; loss and gain; nurturance and neglect; proper ambition and exploitation; and acceptance and change.

Critical dialogues (Gentile and McMillan, 1992) help create a "threshold level of language proficiency" necessary to build the higher order cognition children need to process information for academic purposes and become literate (Cummins, 1984).

These dialogues help create an atmosphere in the classroom geared to inquiry and discovery. To be effective your approach is to encourage ELLs and low language children to:

- Be vigilant, pay attention and focus.
- Think about and begin questioning what they read and write.
- Volunteer responses.
- Listen to one another as well as to you.
- Move to higher levels of thinking and make more thoughtful connections to reading.
- Reduce stress or anxiety toward literacy learning in the regular classroom.

Critical dialogues focus on the literary elements and characters or facts and circumstances in a narrative or expository excerpt that have direct application to the problems or dilemmas children may have encountered in their homes or on the streets.

This complete model can be used effectively with children at Stage V and higher in their language development. Richgels (2002) showed how this type of conversation may occur with children in kindergarten around expository text, but Critical Dialogue is particularly applicable to elementary grades (Ogle, 1986).

> ***Brown, Collins, and Duguid (1989, p.32) said:***
>
> ***By ignoring the situated nature of cognition, education defeats its own goal of providing useable, robust knowledge. Approaches that embed learning in activity and make deliberate use of the social and physical context are more in line with the understanding of learning and cognition that is emerging from research.***

The Instructional Model

Organizing and Framing a Dialogue

1. Identify ground rules for conducting the conversation, i.e., taking turns, not interrupting, following directions and participating.
2. Introduce the literary or informational material and access and develop the children's background knowledge and experiences.

Guiding a Dialogue

1. Identify a significant purpose for reading, listening to or viewing a selection. Solicit a purpose from the children as well.
2. Identify the story line, facts, problem or main idea in the selection. Highlight new information, vocabulary or concepts.
3. Read aloud or ask the children to read a small portion of the selection or view or listen to a portion of a video or audiotape and invite the children to talk about what they were thinking or feeling as they listened, watched or read.

Developing and Expanding a Dialogue

1. After the children listen to, read through or view the selection and talk about their thoughts and feelings, ask them to identify the most important thing they learned about the story or topic, the most important question they have and what difference these ideas or issues make to them.
2. Summarize and clarify the major ideas of the selection and dialogue.
3. Pose meaningful questions and model or demonstrate higher order thinking that includes problem solving, i.e., making inferences or assumptions, forming generalizations and conclusions and interpreting idiomatic or figurative language (metaphor, simile, etc.).
4. Identify contradictions or polarities in the selection.

Multimedia materials such as videos, audio-cassettes or software help reinforce the major ideas or issues that arise during the reading, viewing or dialogue and link these to a character, problem or event that may be familiar and can be used for enrichment.

Closing a Dialogue

Ask the children to write a response to one of the following:

- What is the most important thing you learned from the selection and our conversation?

- What is the most important question you have regarding the selection or our conversation?

- What difference does this make to you?

To be effective in promoting conversation and critical dialogue among ELL children and those struggling to acquire language you:

- Serve as a facilitator to get the children to think about and begin questioning what they read, write, see and hear.

- Enthusiastically present the material in ways that gain and hold the children's attention.

- Respect all the children's attempts to participate in the instructional conversation by honoring their responses and judgments.

- Demonstrate to the children why it is important to listen to one another as well as the teacher.

- Demonstrate higher levels of thinking to show them how to solve problems and analyze or make meaningful connections between what they read, write, see and hear and what they encounter in their daily lives.

- Serve as a model to provide the information and strategies or skills that

help reduce stress or anxiety associated with reading or writing and learning in the classroom (Gentile and McMillan, 1987a).

Example of a Critical Dialogue

Organizing and Framing a Dialogue
Spiders

Materials
Text excerpts: *Spiders & Scorpions, Spiders Spin Silk, Spinning Spiders.*
Story excerpt: *The Very Busy Spider.*
Video Excerpt: National Geographic Video *Spiders.*

Develop an Oracy instructional chart using Ogle's model of K-W-L (1986). Elicit responses from the children: K = What I know.
W = What I want to know. L = What I learned.

Teacher: What do you know about spiders? (List several of the children's responses in the K column on the large butcher paper chart.)

Examples
Spiders make webs.
They can sting you.
Spiders have lots of legs.
They eat flies.

Guiding a Dialogue
Teacher: What do you want to know about spiders? (List several of the children's responses in the W column on the large butcher paper chart.)

Examples
Where do spiders live?
How many legs do they have?
How do they catch their food?
Where do they come from?

After you have charted a few of the children's responses take time to read these to them using a pointer to direct the flow of the text left-to-right. For preschool and kindergarten children use one or two lines of text per page. First and second grade children can work on two or three lines per page. Print their responses in bold black letters and provide ample spacing between words and lines of text.

Developing and Expanding a Dialogue

Use the chart to teach CAP, LAPS, HRSIW and lower strategies of left-to-right directionality, locating known and unknown words and matching one-to-one.

Now, read to the children from an expository text about spiders, e.g., Berman, R. (1998). *Spinning Spiders*. Minneapolis: Lerner Publications; Tainui, B. (2001). *Spiders Spin Silk*. Washington, D.C.: National Geographic Society); or Meadows, G. and Vial, C. (2003). *Spiders & Scorpions*. Pearson Education, Inc., publishing as Dominie Press, an imprint of Pearson Learning Group.

There are many storybooks, informational texts, pictures and videos about spiders available on the Internet.

For children in first or second grade you can use an excerpt (a page or two) from one of these expository texts or an excerpt from another story about spiders (e.g., E.B. White's *Charlotte's Web*) to expand the dialogue. Do shared reading for purposes of developing information processing skills, e.g., identifying main ideas, locating specific facts, sequencing events, critical or creative analysis or summarizing.

Return to the chart and the W column and ask the children which of the things they wanted to learn about spiders were answered in the text. Circle these.

Then ask them, "What is one new fact you learned about spiders? What else do you know?

Closing a Dialogue

Show a snippet (2–3 minutes) of the National Geographic video *Spiders*. Explain to the children that the purpose for watching the video is, "To identify one thing we may have overlooked about spiders in our conversation."

Afterward, ask the children to write a response to one of the following questions:

- What's the most important question you have about spiders?
- What is the most important thing you learned about spiders?
- Why are spiders important to you?
- What do you know now about spiders that you didn't know before we began our work?

Extensive Reading and Writing

While there are many differences among children at each level of language development, those who control the most common structures can learn and accelerate their learning through extensive reading and writing (Ellie and Mangubhai, 1981a, 1981b).

Large blocks of time to read interesting books and compelling material are needed for children acquiring a second language and those whose language experiences away from the classroom may be limited.

Use Sustained Silent Reading (SSR) to generate not just engaged reading but substantial time talking. SSR for 15–25 minutes each day should be coupled with at least 10 minutes devoted to talking about what is read, talking to you

> **Healy (1991, p. 25) said:**
>
> *To read well, minds must be trained to use language, to reflect and persist in solving problems. Students may learn to sound out the words, but unless they possess the internal sense of responsibility for extracting meaning, they are engaging in a hollow, unsatisfying experience. With major effort we have succeeded in teaching students in early grades to 'read the words.' Test scores jump off a cliff, however, when students must begin to plug the words into language meaning and grapple with more advanced grammar, vocabulary and sustained intellectual demands of a real text.*

Children read what they bring to class three days a week. Two days a week they read the same material or excerpts that you select for specific purposes. In both cases you can use the framework for critical dialogue to talk with the children afterward. This provides an effective means of interacting with children after SSR to develop language and literacy instruction. By organizing small groups and teaching them how to analyze text using this approach, you enable them to talk to each other about what they read as you ask:

Extrapersonal Questions (*Responses to these questions are embedded in the text.*)
Who? What? When? Where? How? or Why?

Intrapersonal Questions (*Responses to these questions are embedded in the children's background knowledge and experience.*)
What do you know for sure after reading what you read? What are the facts? (What is true?) What were you thinking and feeling while you were reading? What is the most important question you have about what you read? What is the most important thing you learned from what you read? Do you know someone/something like the person/thing you read about? Write and tell us how this is the same or different.

This approach stimulates children to collaborate with you and with one another to construct meaning from their reading and writing. It also affords you many opportunities to model higher order thinking and motivates children to write using personal experiences to express their thoughts and feelings.

There is ample evidence that reading and writing for long periods of time each day may strengthen both native and non-native speakers' language development, but the relationship is varied and complex (Pickard, 1996).

Reading and writing, especially in the areas of vocabulary and concept development, need to be combined with time spent talking about what is read or written with a competent user of the language (Gray, 1984; Ellie, 1989, 1991).

Extensive reading of simplified and compelling material has also been shown to produce positive gains in second language children's writing (Loban, 1976; Tsang, 1996; Clay, 2002).

Oracy Instruction/Small Groups: Talk/Before-During-After — Stages III-V

- *Introduce "little" commercially published books (story and informational texts) that match interests and language structures children control or partially control for guided reading activities. Focus on vocabulary, comprehension and fluency.*

- *Read Alouds-Think Alouds: Narrative and expository texts. Model fluency, make mental processes audible. Restate, expand and refine children's responses. Use Critical Dialogue to develop vocabulary and comprehension.*

- *Interactive/independent writing: Focus on story reconstruction, narration and informational text. Children work in pairs or independently to write stories or expository texts used for Read-Think Alouds, guided reading or Cloze activities.*

- *Cloze passages activity (hands on): Focus is on Children working in pairs (PSTT) to fill in deleted spaces of a narrative or expository passage to develop vocabulary and comprehension.*

9 Oracy Instruction and Early Intervention
The Role of the Tutor

"If we listened to our intellect, we'd never have a love affair. We'd never have a friendship. We'd never go into business, because we'd be cynical. Well, that's nonsense. You've got to jump off cliffs all the time and build your wings on the way down."

R. Bradbury

It is important to establish language development and literacy behaviors through assessment, direct observation and conversation before beginning early intervention. There are two ways children use language to communicate. Both are important sources of information for tutors working with ELL children and those struggling to acquire oral language.

- Oral language: The structure, vocabulary, intonation, stress, pitch and inflections children use when talking with others (Clay, 1971).

- Self-talk and body language: What children say to themselves and how these internal dialogues affect their responses when learning is stressful (Gentile and McMillan, 1991).

Oral Language
Creating Opportunities for Children to Talk

"Well begun is half done."
M. Monroe

You can use the OLAI as an assessment prior to formal instruction to obtain specific information about a child's stage of oral language development, i.e., expressive speech.

The results provide a benchmark of a child's control over the most common language structures and sentence transformations. The assessment process will reveal strengths as well as confusions regarding verb tense and number as well as story structure, syntax, inflected endings and pronouns.

Determining strengths is as important as identifying what children don't know. Using their strengths to improve language and literacy development rather than focusing on deficits or what they do not control helps maintain a child's interest and motivation for learning.

Using the OLAI will help you:

- Select texts that are a good fit for children's stage of language acquisition and language development.

- Use prompts that help clarify the children's confusions in literacy and enable them to problem solve using meaning, structure and phonemic and visual information at point of error or difficulty to enhance their language and literacy development.

- Engage children in meaningful conversations and create more opportunities for them to talk.

- Interact with the children in ways that foster and link language and literacy development and motivate them to work to overcome difficulties.
- Focus instruction that best meets unique needs in language development necessary to connect to meaning and help accelerate literacy learning.

Children can benefit from preparatory intervention sessions before you move to formal instruction (Clay, 1995). These sessions allow you to establish rapport, administer the OLAI, observe behaviors that support or interfere with language and literacy learning and familiarize children with the interactive processes of working with an adult.

Language and literacy development learning activities corresponding to those of the OLAI should be part of your preparatory sessions. These can include:

- *Talking* about toys and other objects and repeating, expanding or clarifying the children's responses.
- Playing word games and *talking* about them (riddles, jokes, rhymes, tongue twisters, etc.).
- Playing board games and *talking* about them (anagrams, scrabble, etc.).
- Working with puzzles and *talking* with children while you and they are engaged in solving problems of assembling the pieces to complete a mosaic.
- Telling or reading stories and *talking* about them while looking at pictures. Asking children to organize pictures to narrate or tell a logically sequenced story.
- Reading informational texts and *talking* about the topics, vocabulary and concepts or main ideas.
- Sharing experiences and *talking* about them.

- Drawing or painting and *talking* with children before, during and afterward about their illustrations.
- Singing and writing songs and *talking* about them.
- Writing and *talking* about and reading what is written.
- Listening to portions of audiotapes and *talking* about vocabulary, concepts or ideas.
- Watching snippets of videos and *talking* about vocabulary and concepts or ideas.
- Performing an imaginary play and *talking* about the performances.

One of the activities that serve as a bridge to formal lessons involves the use of a disposable camera to make photo albums for reading and writing activities.

Show the children how to use the camera to take pictures of things at school that are important to them (classrooms, friends, the playground, samples of work, the lunchroom, etc.). After you develop the pictures, make a photo album. Have a conversation about the pictures and have the child dictate a sentence for you to write in the album under each one.

You can make other albums by giving a child a disposable camera to take home to photograph family members, pets, activities, playthings, etc. You can take pictures of your family, friends, pets, home, activities, etc. and share the pictures and statements you make.

These albums can be used during preparatory sessions and early lessons to engage children in language development and reading and writing activities.

Pinnell, Lyons, DeFord, Bryk and Seltzer (1994) identified other activities that can be used effectively in tutorial lessons:

- Engaging in familiar, shared or independent reading and writing.
- Identifying sounds and letters.
- Cutting up a child's written sentence, mixing the cut-up words and having the child reassemble the sentence.
- Reading challenging books to make assessments of children's strengths or needs in literacy to guide instruction.

Oracy instruction can be included in your lessons to link language and literacy without compromising the structure of your program. This can be done as you work with children individually or in small groups, in or out of the classroom (see Figure 4, right).

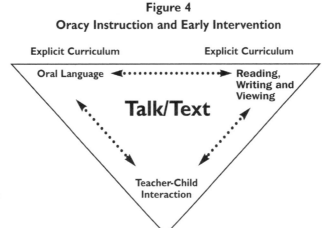

Figure 4
Oracy Instruction and Early Intervention

Connecting Language and Action

The time spent talking with children during tutorial lessons enhances the development of reading and writing skills and strategies and supports accelerated learning.

Encourage children to use whole sentences that connect language and action instead of single-word responses as you move from one activity to the next: "First, I am going to read my favorite books." "Now, I make some words with my letters." "It's time to write my story." "We cut it up and I put it together." "I'll read my new book now."

Rereading
Using Pictures and Language to Construct a Narrative

Every day have a child reread a familiar illustrated book and retell the story, using the pictures to construct a narrative. The child can also read a familiar informational text and answer some questions to stimulate conversation. Start by asking what the child knows about the story or what he or she has learned from reading the text.

If the child struggles with constructing a narrative, look at the first picture and ask some literal level questions, e.g., "Who is playing in the yard?" "What are they doing?" "Who else is there?" "What did you learn about dolphins?" "What do they eat?" Asking some basic questions the child can answer serves as a scaffold for thinking about the story and allows the child to organize information. Sometimes this is all they need to begin "telling" the story. This provides the foundation for making some predictions.

The goal is to have the child talk to you and construct a narrative that contains a logically sequenced beginning, middle and ending, not just name and categorize information. If the child still has difficulty return to the first picture and model a narrative. Provide details or the information needed to create an interesting and enjoyable story. As you turn the pages and point to the pictures, say: "First, this happened…, Then this…, Next this… and, at the end, this happened. Now tell me your story."

The child's narration does not necessarily have to replicate the text but should emphasize the sequence of events and link the pictures with the story.

There is a difference between talking about expository texts and talking about stories. No set sequence is required with exposition, as it usually is with stories (Gentile and McMillan, 1992). When asked to retell or talk about an expository text, a child can begin anywhere, using the most interesting or significant pieces of information to guide and develop a narrative or dialogue. This is especially helpful for developing conversations with children lacking experiences with books and those struggling to acquire language.

After the reading of a familiar story or expository text major teaching points should be vocabulary, comprehension, concept development and fluency. Practice fluency using Line-by-Line Protocol (see pages 28-29).

Recording Progress
Daily Assessment

Every day make a Running Record (Clay, 1993) while the child reads a new book that you introduced and read the day before. In addition to evaluating a child's use of meaning, structure, phonemic or visual cues and problem-solving strategies, record unfamiliar words and concepts in the margin and evaluate the child's level of fluency. You can do this by noting at the bottom of the Running Record Form whether the child read word by word, with some phrasing, or in a smooth, natural cadence.

Including these criteria in the Running Record helps identify the child's strengths and needs in language development and links language and literacy instruction.

After a child reads the Running Record book, identify one or two language development teaching points and processing strategies that require attention. This means talking about and clarifying concepts and specific vocabulary, i.e., important, difficult and interesting or colorful words as well as teaching a child to narrate the story and read fluently.

If the child reads an informational book ask the child to respond to open-ended statements to develop a dialogue. For example, "Tell me what you know for sure after reading this book," "Tell me what you were thinking or feeling while you were reading this book," "Tell me what question(s) you have after reading this," or, "Tell me the most important thing you learned from this book."

When some children with low language development are asked direct questions they may be intimidated because they think they are required to give the "right" answer. But asking them to tell you about something or tell you more about it can free them to respond and may reduce stress and anxiety (Gentile and McMillan, 1987a; 1987b).

This approach can encourage a more positive reaction from children and send a message to them that you really are interested in what they have to say.

If a child is unable to express thoughts or feelings or identify a significant question or point of learning model your own thinking or feelings by talking as you work back through the text. This supports children's efforts to respond (Duffy, Roehler and Hermann (1988); Wood, 1988).

Learning Sounds and Letters
Hearing and Constructing Words and Word Parts

Use plastic magnetic letters to help children identify letters and construct words. This activity can be made into a game you and the children enjoy, such as making rhyming words or words that all begin or end the same way, or seeing how many words you can make with the same group of letters.

Maintain a conversation as you explore differences and similarities. Help the children hear sounds in words and match them to corresponding written symbols.

The ability to hear and locate, not just letter sounds, but also "chunks" and match these to their written counterparts is of single importance in the development of a child's ability to listen, look and locate onsets and rimes (the first and last "chunks" in words) and to identify "how words work" (Clay, 1993; Cunningham, 1995; Good, Kaminski and Smith, 2001).

Letter identification work is often terminated too early in tutorial lessons for children struggling to acquire language. This is one of the main skills supporting the ability to problem solve unfamiliar words in reading and writing. But the meanings of these words have to be clearly established; otherwise, being able to sound them out, write them and construct them is of little value. A child might understand *l/ike b/ike*, but if you ask that child to make *h/ike*, he or she might construct the word but not know what it means.

Making letter identification and word construction meaningful lies in Halliday's (1973) assertion that children do not learn language independently of its functions.

Smith (1975, p. 430) said:

Language to a child always has a use, and the various uses could provide the child a clue to the purposes underlying differences among utterances. A child soon ignores sounds that do not seem to make a difference. There is, in fact, a powerful mechanism in all children preventing them from wasting time on sounds that they can not make sense of, that do not appear to have a purpose; that mechanism is boredom. Even if the strangeness of the sounds initially stimulates their interest, children will not continue to pay attention to sounds that do not make meaningful differences. That is why they grow up speaking language and not imitating the noise of the air conditioner.

Writing
Expanding and Refining Language

It helps to use an unlined 8 1/2 x 11 spiral-bound tablet. Turn the tablet sideways so the child writes across the widest surface on the lower page. The top page can be used to practice writing unfamiliar words, record sounds and letters in words or develop fluent writing.

Use objects, toys or illustrations from a particular text to develop conversations that lead to meaningful writing activities. Talking and thinking about something familiar and tangible, i.e., toys, pictures or experiences, helps engage children in writing activities and establishes an emotional connection that supports meaning and recall.

There is a tendency for children with low language and literacy development to repeat the same familiar structures in their conversations and when dictating and writing "stories." Listen carefully to a child's talk and work to shape dialogue and writing in ways that expand and refine language development. Model and prompt the child to use different nouns, pronouns, verb tenses, vocabulary and language structures (Gentile, 2001). Do this cautiously so the child is not overwhelmed or confused (Clay, 1993).

Encourage children to draw pictures, make statements and tell a story about them. The child can construct pictures and "webs" on a practice page independently or as shared drawing with you. This helps scaffold a conversation, introducing and establishing information, from which to create a brief narrative that forms the basis for writing a "story." Drawing is a major precursor to writing and helps develop hand/eye coordination, visual perception, visual discrimination and spatial organization, all of which are essential to learning to read and write (Brookes, 1986).

It is vital to these children's development of language and literacy that early in their lessons they learn to narrate a story and identify and sequence main ideas as they construct expository text. Otherwise, they may be limited to one- or two-word responses and writing a single simple sentence.

By having children write more complex state-ments or stories and talk about them you support accelerated learning. This helps move them to read texts written at higher levels of difficulty and use more challenging vocabulary and syntax.

Share the writing task with the child. These interactions are important for children to practice hearing and recording sounds in words and letter sequence in word formations. Encourage children to write as much as they can independently but support the writing so the words are written accurately. Use a piece of white tape to cover spelling errors. Then say: "That was almost right, but look." Make sure the child attends as you write on the tape to correct the error. Say the word, ask the child to read it and move on.

Use "sound" boxes (Elkonin, 1971) to introduce a child to writing sounds they hear in one or two of the words they dictate in their sentence or narrative. Select words that have a high sound-symbol correlation, i.e., *sun, pig, bats* or *pop*.

Draw the number of boxes in a sequence to represent each sound in a particular word. Have the children say the word slowly, pronouncing each sound, stretching out the sounds and pushing an index finger into each blank box as they say the sounds slowly. Ask: "What sounds do you hear in this word?" Work steadfastly, having the children repeat the word slowly until the sounds are identified. Then have them write each sound in the corresponding box. (See Clay, 1995 for a complete description of using Elkonin boxes.)

Story Reconstruction and Narrative Comprehension
Sequencing Written Text

Choose one or two statements from the child's dictation and writing and put these on sentence strips. Ask the child to read each word as you cut it off the strip, moving left to right. When you finish cutting up the words spread them out and mix them up in front of the child. Have the child make the sentence. Then ask the child to read it.

This is an effective language and literacy learning activity because in order to reassemble "stories" or sentence(s) a child must be able to search aggressively using language cues: phonemes, graphemes and morphemes. If a child cannot use this information he or she will not be able to secure the "story" in memory, retrieve it and return it to its dictated and written sequence. Moreover, the child is unable to find any meaning in the task of reorganizing cut-up pieces of a "story."

If the child struggles, open up the writing tablet and say: "Make it look just like you wrote it." This provides a scaffold that encourages children to search and cross-check independently to reconstruct their "story" in its original sequence. When the child finishes, work to expand the sentence using a structure word, i.e., preposition, conjunction, relative pronoun or adverb.

Ask the child to expand and refine the sentence using this structure word. For example, the child's "story" is: "We went to the park with my family." To expand the story, prompt the child by asking: "*And* what happened?" or, "*When* did you go to the park?" or, "*Why* did you go to the park?"

Elicit a response. For example, to the prompt "*And*," the child might respond, "*And* we had fun." Then ask the child to "say the whole thing:" "We went to the park with my family *and* we had fun."

The sentence may also be transformed into a negative, a question, a command or an exclamation (Clay, 1971). For example, ask the child, "If you were not able to go to the park, what would you say?" ("We didn't go to the park with my family.") "How could we turn your story into a question?" ("Did we go to the park with my family?") "Or a command?" ("Go to the park with your family.") "Or an exclamation?" (We are going to the park with my family!)

To refine the story ask the child what other word we could use instead of *going*? If the child is unable to identify a synonym say: "We could say, '*We are driving to the park with my family.*'" Acquiring a wide range of vocabulary, i.e., important words, difficult words and colorful or colloquial words is the basis for children's being able to read and write at higher levels (National Reading Panel Report, 2000).

Write only the structure word in a different color on a separate sentence strip frame and place it inside the envelope along with the rest of the child's sentence.

Then write the story the child wrote on the cover of the envelope and send it back to the regular classroom. During journal writing, the child can use the day's sentence or "story" written on the envelope to scaffold independent writing in the journal. The challenge is to look at the sentence, cover it with a card and then write as much as possible from memory.

At point of difficulty, the child can lift the card, look back and cross-check the sentence written on the envelope, replace the card and continue writing. When this is completed, the child opens the envelope, removes the structure word and adds it to the written statement. Then the child finishes independently writing the expansion of the "story" that was dictated to you in the lesson at the close of the writing activity. An additional challenge is to try to write the

Oracy Instruction and Early Intervention: The Role of the Tutor

synonym used to refine the sentence (*driving*) using invented spelling.

The classroom teacher should have an expanded "word wall" (100–125 words) that children can use as a reference for writing high frequency words correctly.

Introducing New Material

Selecting a Book

The choice of a new book is critical for children with low language development. Children should be able to independently read 90 percent of the text you select (Clay, 1991a). Choose new books taking into consideration sociocultural experiences, interests, background knowledge, vocabulary and language structures children control or partially control.

Balance the number of narrative texts with an assortment of expository texts. Expository text exposes children to language needed to *talk* about real things in their physical and social environments. These books can entertain as well as educate. They can be used to teach content vocabulary, concepts and more about "how the world works."

Introducing the Book

Let the child look through the book and *talk* about the story or information presented in the pictures. You can encourage interaction by asking questions and commenting on the child's observations (see Clay, 1991b). Prompt the child by saying: "Say more about that." "Tell me more."

Then you *talk* about the story or information focusing on meaning and language development. Make sure the child *talks* as

much or more than you do. The goal should be to provide opportunities for the child to narrate the text using the pictures and language to establish meaning rather than just label, classify or categorize information.

During the introduction it is always advisable to rehearse new language structures and discuss important, difficult or colorful vocabulary and concepts. One way to rehearse a new language structure is to identify it in the text, close the book, say it, then ask the child to repeat it. Then reopen the book and have the child read that sentence.

Introduce an unfamiliar word in the context of a whole sentence by restating what the child has narrated using the new word. Use both visual and auditory prompts. Ask the child what letter(s) would you expect to see at the beginning of that word? Have the child look at the beginning of the word and identify the first letter or letters and think about a familiar word that makes sense and would fit. You can also have the child sound

Clay (1991, p.69) said:

If the child's language development seems to be lagging it is misplaced sympathy to do his talking for him. Instead put your ear closer, concentrate more sharply, smile more rewardingly and spend more time in genuine conversation, difficult though it is. To foster children's language development, create opportunities for them to talk, and talk with them (not at them).

it out, searching left to right identifying sound and letter sequences. But just sounding out a word is not always a reliable strategy and certainly does not guarantee comprehension so spending time talking about the meaning of the word in context is essential.

Reading the New Book

After introducing the book have the child read. Prompt the child to use these problem-solving strategies when necessary. Do a second reading of the new book to practice unfamiliar language structures, words and fluency.

Stress and Language and Literacy Development

"There is nothing good or bad, but thinking makes it so."

W. Shakespeare

Stress plays a critical role in language and literacy development (Gentile and McMillan, 1987a). Stress affects the ability of children to focus and process, store or retrieve information (Perry, 1997).

Many children requiring intervention live in poverty or violence and are isolated and neglected (Perry, 1999). Critical life events may adversely affect their social-emotional and intellectual development (Gentile, McMillan and Swain, 1985; Lyons, 1999). A parent, or both parents, may have died or abandoned them. Some are "latchkey" children left to fend for themselves. Others are the products of broken or dysfunctional homes—children who have been shifted from one family member to another or moved in and out of foster care. Still others are homeless, living in shelters, vehicles or on the streets.

Some come from homes where parents apply strict discipline when their children do not make satisfactory progress in school or fail to behave according to a set of "rules" the parents have established. On the other hand, there are parents who overprotect their children and "sacrifice" everything for them, often at great cost to themselves or other family members. Other parents reject their youngsters' efforts, always anticipating failure or comparing them unfavorably to themselves or siblings.

These children may experience an inordinate amount of stress when learning is difficult for them. When this happens they feel threatened and have not learned to cope successfully. Their negative self-talk disrupts and presents a barrier to learning. They perceive what is expected of them to be beyond their control (Gentile and McMillan, 1991). Because of their stress responses (fight/flight) during instruction children who struggle with language and literacy development are often Hard to Reach and Hard to Teach. Your observations and interactions are crucial in teaching them new coping skills.

Dreikurs (1954, p. 340) said:

To understand a child in his functions and performances, one must keep in mind that man is a social animal, a zoon politico (Aristotle). Since he functions entirely within a social atmosphere, all his functions and performances have social significance. To understand a child requires comprehension of his total personality within his social setting. It is impossible to blame any one factor in the child's makeup for his behavior or deficiencies.

Self-Talk and Body Language: Working With Hard to Reach Hard to Teach Children

"Empathic listening is so powerful because it gives you accurate data to work with. Instead of projecting your own autobiography and assuming thoughts , feelings, motives and interpretation, you're dealing with the reality inside another person's head and heart. You're focused on receiving the deep communication of another soul."

S. Covey

Self-talk reveals the nature of a child's internal dialogue when faced with a problem. While administering the OLAI it is important to observe whether the child appears flexible, frustrated, immobilized or helpless when learning is difficult because these responses are fueled by self-talk.

When children perceive learning as stressful they may try to avoid or escape the source of their discomfort. These "fight or flight" responses tend to reinforce themselves because they reduce anxiety. Such responses are difficult to change but you cannot manage what you don't observe and measure.

Listen to what a child says that may reveal any negative self-talk and observe the child's bearing while working with you. Compare your observations with the classroom teacher and parents. Identify related responses using the Stress Response Scale for Language and Literacy Development (see Page 56) to strengthen your observations.

Your challenge is to address negative self-talk through instructional interactions in ways that help alter a child's perception of learning as being stressful or threatening, i.e., "too hard," "unpleasant," "tedious," or "debilitating." (Gentile and McMillan, 1987a). While many children lead stressful lives at home and in school, they still need to acquire language and literacy to lead productive and fulfilling lives. "But it may take more time and patience and calling them disabled is hardly likely to help (Smith, 2003 p. 13)."

The Stress Response Scale for Language and Literacy Development

"If you are distressed by anything external, the pain is not due to the thing itself but to your own estimate of it; and this you have the power to revoke at any moment."

M. Aurelius

The Stress Response Scale for Language and Literacy Development is a useful supplement to the OLAI and other measures of reading and writing proficiency. Language and literacy assessment needs to be multidimensional and ongoing.

The results of this scale are helpful in designing effective intervention that focuses attention on teaching coping behaviors as much as on teaching strategies and skills.

Scoring the Scale

To determine flexible responses, count the number of *a*'s; count the number of *b*'s to identify the fight responses; flight responses are reflected by the number of *c*'s (see Page 56).

Typically, one pattern will dominate although there can be a mixture of reactions. Even when one response pattern is not dominant, the information can still be used to design more effective interactions and individualized intervention.

Children who respond flexibly when challenged use positive self-talk and try different strategies or skills to solve problems. They are resilient, can tolerate ambiguity and cope successfully with adversity. These children generally control the language of instruction and do not require special intervention.

Intervention

"Both the dreamer and the child who seeks attention through aggression may have reading problems. One is seeking escape from this insolvable problem and the other is trying to compensate for his feelings of inferiority. The teacher who is able to help these children must have a deep interest in them and a great amount of patience."

L. Knowles

After you have determined the pattern of a child's stress responses the next step is to plan appropriate intervention.

When children demonstrate fight/flight or avoidant responses, it is important to understand the types of interactions that may take place between you and them (see Figure 5, Page 55, and Figure 6, Page 59).

The way you are teaching reflects how you respond to Hard to Reach Hard to Teach Children. It is not uncommon for you to feel "stressed" or threatened. Deci (1985) presented

Clay (1993, p. 57) cautioned:

You may decide that you have to work out some new ways of getting the child to do the 'reading work' in the areas in which he is opting out... Often he has learned to do something which is interfering with his progress, and he may have learned it from the way you are teaching.

research pointing to some broader effects of stress in language and literacy learning. Deci's studies showed that teachers are under excessive pressure to increase children's standardized achievement test scores. Deci, et al. (1982) indicated that stress produced by this pressure makes teachers more controlling than they know they should be.

The additional mandates of current professional performance and achievement standards for English Language Learners and children with low language development increase the pressure some teachers feel and have the potential to elicit even more rigidity and control.

Fight Responses

Some children have a low frustration tolerance and respond impulsively or rigidly to language and literacy tasks. These children may avoid reading and writing by confronting you, thus leaving the work behind. A child might also respond in rigid ways and "fight" to be perfect or to get things just right. In the first instance, the child confronts or fights the teacher and the work. On the other hand, the child who is

The Oracy Instructional Guide
Oracy Instruction and Early Intervention: The Role of the Tutor

Figure 5
Stress Responses When Learning Is Difficult

Flexible Response	**Fight Response**	**Flight Response**
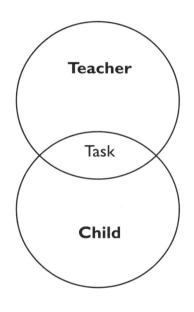	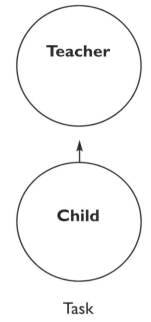	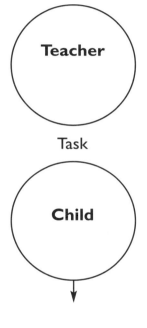
The child interacts positively with the teacher, approaches and focuses on the tasks.	The child confronts the teacher or the task to avoid the work.	The child flees from the task and interaction with the teacher or the task.

The Stress Response Scale

"The education of the will is the object of our existence."   R. W. Emerson

The Stress Response Scale for Language and Literacy Development (Gentile and McMillan, 1987) should be used only as an observational tool and guide. It helps measure and identify a child's pattern of self-talk and resultant behavior that may interfere with accelerated learning. This scale can be used to raise your awareness of the differences in the way children respond to tasks when they perceive them to be difficult.

Because of the complexity of social-emotional factors in language and literacy acquisition, these responses are difficult to categorize precisely. The scale is not intended to *label* children; instead, it is designed to provide an overall impression of a child's responses. The results are not all-inclusive; they suggest behavioral trends or patterns.

For each of the following phrases, circle the letter, *a, b,* or *c,* depending on which phrase most accurately describes a child's responses to language and literacy instruction at the point of difficulty, confusion, or error. The letter *a* = approach / flexible responses, *b* = avoidant / fight responses, and *c* = avoidant / flight responses.

1. a. tries different strategies
   b. becomes rigid and quits searching
   c. becomes anxious or apprehensive

2. a. asks questions related to difficulty or confusion
   b. acts out feelings of frustration, defiance, or anger
   c. appears insecure or fearful

3. a. relaxes, appears confident and reflective
   b. responds impulsively to prompts, engages in random searching
   c. appears subdued, withdrawn, or depressed

4. a. engages in a dialogue with the teacher to confirm or reject a response
   b. cries, throws tantrums
   c. seeks rescue through overly appellate behavior

5. a. is self-deprecating in a positive way and appears unruffled
   b. appears rigid or perseverates, piling error on error
   c. appears passive and unable to focus or concentrate

6. a. is open to suggestions to redirect attention or efforts
   b. becomes defensive, verbalizes attitude, "I don't want to."
   c. appears timid, verbalizes attitude, "I can't. It's too hard."

7. a. accepts challenges, works flexibly to problem solve
   b. seeks amusement, shows little tolerance for ambiguity or challenge
   c. takes no risks, answers, "I don't know," even when the answer is obvious

8. a. is accommodating, follows directions, fulfills expectations
   b. resists compliance, does not follow directions or fulfill expectations
   c. daydreams or frets over lack of ability

9. a. adapts to change in routines, takes risks
   b. is upset by change, attempts to manipulate the situation to personal aims
   c. requires constant assurance, "Did I get that right?" "Was that good?"

10. a. engages in daily work willingly
    b. is disruptive, seeks to deviate from work
    c. expresses fear or rejection for perceived deficiencies

11. a. works independently and concentrates
    b. makes excuses for lack of participation; temporizes or stalls
    c. appears immobilized when asked to work independently

12. a. engages in appropriate, meaningful conversation with teacher
    b. makes sarcastic, bizarre, or nonsensical comments or "weird" sounds
    c. becomes excessively self-critical, "I'm dumb," "I'll never get it right."

13. a. laughs easily, appears to enjoy reading, writing, and problem solving
    b. bursts into loud, raucous laughter, declares work is "no fun," "boring"
    c. appears apathetic or disinterested; doesn't try

overly self-critical is unwilling to accept imperfection and may perseverate, i.e., repeat the same thing over and over.

Fight responses present interesting challenges to you as a teacher and can seriously test your patience and determination. It is helpful to do "the second thing that comes to mind." This is wise because the first response you are apt to make to children acting out, attempting to manipulate the lesson or interfering with the pace of instruction is fueled by *emotion*. Reactive, emotional responses on your part are counterproductive and relinquish control to the child.

Be firm, resolute and consistent – but talk less. Over-talking at fight behavior provides more opportunity for a child to control the focus and pace of the lesson, your responses and the amount of work expected and completed.

When you work with children who exhibit fight responses, try to channel behavior so the energy used to distract or deviate from instruction or at getting everything just right is redirected to language and literacy development. This requires intervention using firm, explicit modeling, a call to attention and less talk. When working with fight responses aimed at perfection, it may also

> *Gentile and McMillan (1987a, p.21) said:*
>
> **The fight response has a force behind it that, when managed well, is advantageous for working to overcome language and literacy difficulties. The flight response is characterized by learned helplessness, inertia or apathy and contains no such force.**

mean less correction of error and some lighthearted humor.

For example, when a child engages in deviant behavior, acts out or is resistive to reading and writing instruction, say something like this: "Stop. What you are doing is not helping you. This is what you need to do to help yourself. When you feel you don't want to do what you need to do, I want you to say to yourself: 'I am going to do this. I am not going to get angry, frustrated, act silly or throw a tantrum. I need to think about what I know that can help me and go back and see if it works. If it doesn't, I'll try something else.' Now watch and listen to me as I show and explain what to do, then you do the same thing."

On the other hand, fight responses related to a child's need to get things "right" or to be perfect require a different approach. Instead of confronting you or the task, the child tends to be excessively self-critical. It is not unusual to observe children slapping themselves, pounding their forehead with their hands or banging their fists or head on the desk when they think they have made an error.

Helping these children to accept some imperfection, relax, take risks and have some fun with you is essential to their learning to work more flexibly.

When a child persists in doing the same thing that does not help overcome difficulty you can say: "You know, I've made that mistake before. Here's what I say to myself. Here's what I do. There's nothing wrong with making an error or being confused. I can do… to help myself or ask someone to help me. Usually I take a couple of deep breaths and then I try something different. If that doesn't work, I can try something else. This keeps me going so I don't get stuck."

While fight responses are challenging, working with impulsive or rigid fight behavior can sometimes be less taxing than working with children who exhibit learned helplessness or flight behavior.

Flight Responses

The flight response results from children's fear of failure or learned helplessness. They have not learned to take risks to improve performance. They retreat when challenged and may have learned that adults do not expect them to be competent.

Many adults respond to learned helplessness through lowered expectations and try to "rescue" children by taking over a task or terminating it. These adult responses may stem from misplaced sympathy, and they reinforce flight behavior (Clay, 1991). Ultimately, they free children from having to take responsibility for their own learning.

Many children have developed flight behaviors when tasks are even minimally difficult. Your challenge is to scaffold their efforts so they acquire coping skills that allow them to approach learning when it is difficult. Supportive interactions with these children help foster confidence and competence.

Arranging manageable, incremental steps helps reduce the amount of anxiety these children experience while working with you. This gives them time and helps them learn to reconstruct negative thoughts and self-talk. Gradually they can assume responsibility for their own learning.

This requires intervention using explicit modeling and prompts such as: "When you get

Manzo (1987, p. 409) said:

Whenever anyone is distressed it creates a preoccupation with the emotionally charged issue which in turn causes disruption of clear thinking, perception and not surprisingly test like performance. 'Common sense psychology' also suggests that when learning does not become generative, that is, beginning to roll along and grow between instructional periods, the child clearly is not thinking about, rehearsing and applying what has been taught. Ultimately, all learning has to become self determined or it simply will not occur in any profound way.

stuck, here's what I want you to say to yourself. 'I can do this. I need to slow down and think of what I can try that will help me. If I don't know what to do, I'll ask for help.' Now watch and listen to me and you'll be able to do what I do. If you need help, I'll help you."

In the flight response children learn they don't have to try if they don't want to or when something is challenging or difficult. With reduced expectations these children give up or surrender easily. They are deprived of opportunities to learn "optimism" and the development of self-esteem that comes from working to resolve problems (Seligman, 1998).

The absence of motivation, i.e., energy or desire, makes working with flight responses

Figure 6
Coping Styles of Children Who Perceive Learning Tasks as Threatening

	Fight	Flight
Child's Self-talk	"I won't do this and you can't make me."	"I can't do this and no one can help me."
Stress Responses	Ridicules participation, reading, writing, books, the teacher, and school Confronts teacher to avoid learning Perseverates; rigid and inflexible Anxiety and energy directed outward Defiant, yells or becomes hostile, obstinate and resistive; acts out feelings by having tantrums, throwing objects and resisting Moves past the task to disrupt, deter, or distract the teacher	Criticizes self Retreats into fantasy, silence, or daydreams, moving away from the teacher as well as the task Anxiety and energy turned inward Cries, pouts, or appears sad, despondent, or helpless; whines, quits easily Withdraws and does little to approach the task independently; tries to gain sympathy and help by "proving" inadequacies; requires constant supervision and guidance
Teacher's Stress Response	Generally, the teacher becomes involved in a power struggle with the child.	Generally, the teacher tries to "rescue" the child.

Oracy Instruction and Early Intervention: The Role of the Tutor

especially difficult. Figure 6 (Page 59) illustrates children's different coping styles, patterns of internal dialogue and stress responses, along with the typical teacher responses prior to intervention.

Effective intervention in these children's language and literacy learning must combine not only strategic text processing skills, but must also take into account teaching children the appropriate behavior to solve problems and a belief in their ability.

There is a difference between possessing skills and strategies and being able to apply them under stressful circumstances. This requires children who struggle to acquire language and literacy to develop self-regulatory coping strategies.

Without these strategies, most children behave in counterproductive ways to reduce anxiety. These self-defeating, habituated behaviors serve to expunge the "threat" that reading and writing pose, whether it be the loss of self-esteem, frustration, fear or ridicule.

Children can learn to cope when you prompt them to reappraise the level of threat, model explicit coping strategies and hold them accountable (Hilgard, Atkinson and Atkinson, 1975; Blackham and Silberman, 1980).

Self-defeating behavior can be altered by providing positive, incremental successful experiences and changing negative self-talk.

A child demonstrating fight or flight behaviors during language and literacy instruction benefits from learning three major self-regulatory coping strategies: goal setting, self-incentives and self-monitoring (Bandura, 1977; Kanfer, 1980; Runck, 1982; Clay, 2001).

Goal Setting, Incentives and Self-Monitoring

"When people commit themselves to explicit goals, negative discrepancies between what they do and what they seek to achieve serve as motivators for change. By making self-satisfaction contingent on goal attainment, people persist in their efforts until their attainments match what they are seeking to achieve."   A. Bandura

The purpose of many instructional activities may appear unclear, meaningless or overly difficult to children who struggle with language and literacy acquisition.

Learning to read and write may be unrelated to some children's goals and provide no evidence of overcoming personal or educational difficulties. In fact, these activities may only highlight their perceived incompetencies (Gentile and McMillan, 1987a).

You can work more successfully with these children by helping them establish explicit goals and by providing immediate performance feedback. Goal setting along with performance feedback can be highly effective in developing self-motivation and improving performance.

Neither goals without performance feedback nor performance feedback without goals achieves any lasting change (Bandura and Cervone, 1984).

The degree to which establishing goals is an incentive for self-directed change is dependent on three things: the explicitness of the goals, the level of the goals and the proximity of the goals.

Goal Setting

The Explicitness of the Goals

Explicit goals provide clear guides for action as well as the means for children and tutors to evaluate performance. General goals are too vague and fail to direct children's motivation and behavior.

The Level of the Goals

Setting reasonable goals, working through incremental instructional steps and making conservative appraisals of achievement sustain children's motivation and self-directed change. Unrealistic goals can lead to a loss of trust and reinforce feelings of incompetence.

The Proximity of the Goals

The effectiveness of the goals is largely determined by how far into the future they are projected. Short term goals mobilize effort and direct what one does now. While long term goals are important, focusing on the future makes it too easy to temporize efforts at change in the present.

If children have short term goals for improving their language and literacy acquisition each day, in the time it takes to complete an intervention program, they will be well on the road to attaining their long-term goals.

Incentives

"In human effort the only source of energy is desire." S. Weil

Another important step in developing children's initial coping and self-regulating behavior is to help them identify incentives and rewards for reaching established goals.

These can be highly individual and often surprising in their simplicity. It is important to take the time to define each child's incentives.

Bandura, (1985, pp. 10-11) said:

One can always begin in earnest in the tomorrows of each day. Your challenge is to help a child establish short term goals that can realistically be accomplished. These subgoals are the basis for greater achievement in the future. They also provide continuous incentives and guides for self regulation that build a sense of competence, self satisfaction and motivation.

While some incentives can be used effectively for groups of children, the most powerful and sustaining are those identified by the children themselves.

Ultimately, there is a big difference between developing intrinsic motivation to be an effective reader and writer and being extrinsically motivated to read and write by rewards or punishments from teachers, parents or peers.

Self-Monitoring

"Most powerful is he who has himself in his own power." Seneca the Younger

As a final step in children's acquisition of coping and self-regulatory skills you can help them learn to self-monitor behaviors they need to change in order to become effective readers and writers. Encouraging children to observe and identify the level of stress and events that foster it serves several purposes. When children observe their behavior and the circumstances under which it occurs, they can use their observations to identify and monitor what causes particular behaviors that need to be changed. Self-monitoring also provides necessary information for setting realistic subgoals and for evaluating progress.

Sports provide a model for demonstrating the importance of self-monitoring. A weightlifter, for example, can record the increasing number of presses or curls and can see increased muscle mass. This positive feedback encourages continued effort and improvement (Horn, 1986). You can set up the same kind of circumstances by establishing incremental checkpoints for children across time in their language and literacy development.

Helping children observe and mark these incremental gains provides positive feedback. To ensure long-term effects, children who struggle with language and literacy development must have reasons to change that make sense to them and they must have the means to bring about that change.

Many children who struggle with language acquisition and reading and writing may not have developed flexible problem-solving skills. They tend to use a singular approach to problem solving, even when it does not produce a positive result, i.e., when their attempts fail,

they do more of the same, heaping error upon error (Entwisle, 1971; Wood, 1988).

Before positive changes can occur, children must recognize their behavioral difficulties, acknowledge the nature of them and gain control using adaptive stress-reducing behaviors. This means sizing up the level of challenge or threat accurately and learning to take risks. In order to do so, children need to take positive action when they are stuck or confused, or when they make errors, and develop the following specific literacy problem-solving strategies:

- Search for information in word sequences, meaning and letter sequences.
- Discover new things for themselves and ask for help when they need it.
- Cross-check information, using at least two sources.
- Learn to reread in order to confirm meaning and make what they read make sense by reading what the author wrote.
- Take the initiative to check the accuracy of what they read or write.
- Monitor their own reading and writing.
- Read and write words accurately, using all these means (Askew and Fountas, 1997).

Becoming effective readers and writers requires much more than learning how to "sound out" unknown words. In essence, children must learn to work at difficulty, take some initiative and make connections to something they already know (Clay, 1993).

Interactions

"Put yourself wholeheartedly into something and energy grows. It seems inexhaustible. If, on the other hand, you are divided or conflicted about what you are doing, you create anxiety. And the amount of physical and emotional energy consumed by stress or anxiety is exorbitant." H. De Rosis, M.D.

Your interactions with these children are crucial for helping them change their negative perceptions of learning. As previously discussed, this is accomplished in part by explicit modeling, supporting children in developing attainable goals, providing consistent feedback at the right time and eliciting self-evaluative information directed at their efforts to employ problem-solving strategies and skills.

A *structured* approach is vital to successful intervention and helping them learn effective coping and self-regulatory strategies.

Research on learned helplessness indicates that, with few exceptions, many problems in language and literacy acquisition arise from lack of targeted effort rather than lack of ability (Clay, 1986; Seligman, 1998). Thus, the issue is not whether you can always prevent adversity or stress during instruction, but how you help children cope when it occurs.

Immediate and continued success is essential for these children, but your challenge is to gradually show them they can successfully cope with fear and anxiety when learning is difficult. It is important for them to acknowledge and

accept these feelings but not to let fear or anxiety control them. Anxiety feeds on itself. Recognizing the source, putting it into perspective and sharing concerns with you are the first steps to stress reduction. Then children can become less frustrated, passive and vulnerable and more able to cope. These "approach" experiences and interactions help get rid of self-destructive or distorted thinking.

The concepts of "goodness of fit" and "poorness of fit" can guide and shape your interactions with children when difficulties arise. Goodness of fit occurs when your instructional materials, approach and expectations are in concert with children's capacities, interests, motivations and values. A good fit leads to success as measured by their knowledge of strategies and skills and how to apply them, i.e., of knowing what to do when they are stuck and exerting themselves to try to resolve problems. A good fit also produces other positive attitudes and behavior changes during instruction.

By contrast, a poor fit involves conflict between the children's instructional materials, approaches and expectations. Stress that occurs because of a poor fit between these factors and children's fight or flight responses may trigger or exacerbate social and emotional interference during instruction.

When this happens, children develop a negative perception of language and literacy acquisition and of themselves as readers and writers geared to failure. They may expect to do poorly and fail; consequently they do both. Their apprehension makes them anxious enough to force these outcomes.

Your relationship and studied interactions with these children are the keys to working successfully. This requires patience, understanding, forbearance and knowledge. Ultimately you can help them use their strengths to overcome weaknesses and achieve individual goals as well as those established for learning in the regular classroom. Knowing what to say and when to say it, what not to say or when to remain silent, what to do and what not to do, how much to help and when to get out of the way and let the child do the work is the *sine qua non* of good teaching.

Self-Assessment

"Self reverence, self knowledge, self control. These three alone lead life to sovereign power." A. Lord Tennyson

A frequently overlooked component of language and literacy assessment is self-assessment. Your mediation process, self-talk and belief system are as crucial to the success of intervention as those of the children with whom you work.

Consider what happens when you experience stress as you work with these children. They are particularly sensitive and vulnerable to your behavior and responses. It is imperative that you try to make sure your frustrations do not interfere with teaching and learning and thereby exacerbate an already stressful situation for many of these children (Deci, et al., 1982).

Working with these children can be stressful for several reasons:
- They may not always make us look or feel good as teachers or tutors and, in the absence of required training or a framework for working effectively with them, we feel vulnerable and may demonstrate fight or flight responses ourselves.
- We may be increasingly aware that their difficulties or failure to demonstrate measurable progress or accelerated learning could reflect unfavorably on our professional evaluation or reputation.
- We may dislike or resent working with these children because their resistance and helplessness reveal our inability to work successfully with them and challenge us beyond learned and practiced teaching and coping skills.
- To be successful we have to change our thinking and belief systems and change the way we teach and interact with these children. And change, in these situations, may be demanding and long-term.

As a measure of your capacity to provide a good instructional fit for these children, and as a focus for your self-assessment and growth, it will help for you to work over time to be able to answer the following questions affirmatively.
- Do I enjoy learning?
- Have I learned to do at least one new thing in the past year?
- Do I enjoy reading and writing, and do I read and write regularly for personal as well as professional purposes?
- Do I spend as much or more time reading and writing as I do watching television each week?
- Do I enjoy teaching children who are hard to teach or reach?
- Do I understand and believe that low language acquisition is a major impediment to a child's learning to read and write and that effective instruction must integrate language and literacy learning?

- Do I believe this child can learn to read and write at the expected level?
- Do I believe I can help this child achieve that level?
- Do I want to work with this child?
- Do I look forward to going to work every day?

A negative answer to even one of these questions can be a source of teacher or tutor stress that, if unresolved, creates barriers to successful intervention, no matter how well it is designed.

Helping children develop their language and cope with stress to become effective readers and writers can be especially rewarding. Learning and applying coping skills not only has the potential to improve children's well-being, but it also adds to yours.

> **Blackham and Silberman (1980, p. 44) said:**
>
> **Opportunities to perform desired activities are used to reinforce infrequently performed responses. In this sense, we can say that reinforcing responses (rather than reinforcing stimuli) increase the frequency or strength of the desirable responses. For example, when a child is permitted to engage in behavior B, the opportunity to perform behavior A reinforces behavior B. Behavior is maintained or changed as a result of its consequences; that is, behavior is a function of reinforcement.**

Ultimately, you serve as a resolute, enthusiastic model for these children. You demonstrate learning how to read and write and the value of becoming a good reader and writer. Most importantly you show them how to make adjustments or change behavior that interferes with or blocks learning.

This requires self-knowledge and self-control and suggests a broader definition of teacher training. The words *improvise, adapt* and *overcome* provide an excellent rubric for guiding tutorial work with these children. This indicates an ability and willingness to respond flexibly in stressful circumstances.

Flexible Intervention for Hard to Reach Hard to Teach Children

"When you're in a rut, see what others are doing that is different. Don't become discouraged when things don't go as you plan. Keep your enthusiasm, but temper it with self-discipline and maturity. Realize some things just come with experience."

R. McKnight, third grade teacher, Henderson, Tennessee

The following general steps have been shown to be effective for instructional intervention with individuals and groups of children whose responses to reading and writing are fight or flight (Gentile and McMillan, 1987).

The tutor and child:
- Agree on an accurate description of behaviors that interfere with or impede learning.

- Clearly establish the need and purpose for change.
- Establish a time frame for accomplishing purposes and goals for language development and reading and writing achievement.
- Identify and define specific incentives for language and literacy improvement.
- Develop a contingency management plan that includes those things or experiences the child identifies as being important, valuable and worth working for.

Contingency management has a long history of being effective in changing children's behavior because reinforcing conditions take the form of events, privileges, interests or activities.

The chance to do what one would like to do is a generally accepted motivational tool. A low probability behavior can be reinforced by the opportunity to engage in a high probability behavior. Many parents have used this principle successfully with such directives as: "When you finish such-and-such, you can do such-and-such."

The tutor designs and provides:
- Incremental instructional steps for learning that permit the child to succeed immediately and over time. Putting this information in the form of a written contract for children and parents is helpful.
- Consistent feedback for children, classroom teachers and parents on the child's strategies and skills in language acquisition and reading and writing, self-regulatory or coping skills and positive behavioral changes during instruction.

Observational information, the results of the Stress Response Scale for Language and Literacy Development and a contingency management plan can help you intervene successfully with children's avoidant behaviors and negative self-talk.

Approaches to Change Fight or Flight Responses

Step 1: General Approach
Establish a set of ground rules, identify and describe:
- Your responsibilities.
- The child's responsibilities.
- What you expect to do each day and how it will be done.
- What the child is expected to do each day and how it will be done.
- Jointly constructed consequences when goals for lessons are or are not reached.

Variations for Fight Responses
Be consistent, clear, firm and direct. Focus your interactions directly on the instructional conversation. Provide limited choices at first. Accept and honor approximations; praise and encourage the child, but hold the child accountable for following ground rules and directions and self-monitoring during instruction. Provide consistent reinforcement for incremental levels of the child's language and literacy achievement and positive behavioral adjustments.

Variations for Flight Responses
Discuss the child's feelings of inadequacy. Try to be objective and nonjudgmental. Listen empathically but avoid the "sympathy trap." Provide directions and model explicit strategies, positive, flexible and effective self-talk and strategies for managing fear or anxiety. Then ask the child to role-play and talk out loud while working to solve a problem.

To be successful in school and life after school, children must learn to be persistent, to take risks and not give up easily. They must learn to take responsibility for their actions, face challenges and develop strategies and skills to solve problems.

Step 2: General Approach

Describe the purposes and goals for language and literacy development and the incremental steps or components of a typical lesson.

- Our purposes each day for working together are…
- These are important because…
- You will have this much time to finish this much work…
- If you finish what we have to do each day, you can…

Ask the child to repeat:
- The purposes and goals.
- Why the purposes and goals are important.
- How much time is allowed for completing each day's work.
- The contingency plan, i.e., consequences when purposes and goals for lesson are or are not reached.

Variations for Fight Responses

At the point where a child's behavior adversely affects learning and concentrated effort, say: "Stop. We decided what your job is each day and talked about how you would work. This behavior is unacceptable. Now listen and watch me as I do what you are going to do. Then, you do what I do." Your message to the child is: "You can do this. I'll never ask you to do anything you can't do, and it's to your advantage to do it. When we finish, this is what will happen for you." These terms are not negotiable.

In the case of the child who insists on perfection, establish a more flexible set of ground rules and expectations to avoid the child's tendencies to do everything just right or to adhere to a rigid standard of performance.

Variations for Flight Responses

Explain that some things the child will have to do may be difficult, but you will never ask the child to do more than is possible. Make it clear that when the work becomes challenging you will provide assistance. But you expect the child to try to overcome difficulty using a strategy or skill you teach.

Your focus is on encouraging and expecting the child to try something when learning is difficult. If the child struggles, model the strategy or skill. Then turn the work over to the child.

The amount of time needed to complete more challenging activities can be adjusted.

Your message to the child is: "The surest way not to succeed is not to try." Say: "Sometimes, we are afraid to try because we worry we will fail. This is not going to happen. I will help you succeed. We will work together, but you are responsible for doing your part. When you finish, this is what you can expect." The terms for working with these children can be more flexible.

Step 3: General Approach

Model appropriate behaviors for successfully applying a strategy or skill.

Your focus is on demonstrating how to respond effectively to difficult or stressful situations and what you say to yourself as you work.

Variations for Fight Responses

Talk to the child about what went well during the lesson and confirm the child's ability to do the work you have established. Your focus is to move the problem-solving task into the foreground. If the child attempts to divert your attention, remain steadfast and resolute. Fight responses are often the result of a child's impulsivity or propensity for diversion and amusement.

Model appropriate coping behaviors. Identify and describe each step in the problem-solving process and what you say to yourself as you work through them. Then, hold the child accountable for doing what you do. Honor and praise approximations, but demonstrate the process again. Then ask the child to try again. Do this until the child succeeds.

For those children who are highly self-critical, model relaxation techniques, e.g., taking a couple of deep breaths when learning is difficult and trying a couple of different strategies or skills that you have taught. Demonstrate these if necessary, then ask the child to do the same. Praise and encourage the child's effort. Help the child learn to take a less worrisome or perfect approach to solving problems.

Variations for Flight Responses
Model the problem-solving process, but break it down incrementally and ask the child to do each part after you do it. Talk while you do this, explaining your thinking. When each step has been completed, ask the child to do the whole process. When necessary, scaffold the child's efforts but have the child work with you to complete the action. This provides a "safety net" that helps reduce a child's anxiety and encourages risk taking. Ultimately this leads to working independently.

Step 4: General Approach
Design and implement your lessons so they incorporate vocabulary development, comprehension and fluency as well as word identification.

Variations for Fight Responses
Move the child to the day's work without delay. Focus on meaning as the child reads or writes. Honor and praise appropriate reading and writing behavior. Selection of materials and activities is critical. If the child is uninterested in a particular book or writing activity, this

provides fuel for the child to distract you or disrupt the lesson. Provide opportunities for the child to use background knowledge and experiences to talk about words and meanings with you, but move directly back to the work.

From time to time, ask the child to narrate a story or text using the pictures. Add details that are overlooked, but keep the narrative moving forward. If the child struggles, model self-talk and problem-solving approaches. Afterward, practice reading fluently with patterned text for a few minutes, using "Line-by-Line Protocol" (see pages 28-29).

Share the pen in writing as much as needed to maintain the flow. Insist on the child doing the work. Focus on the child's interests in writing. Offer a choice between two topics. Use a practice page for the child to attempt writing unfamiliar words independently and clarify as needed.

Keep the lesson moving at a lively, focused pace. Praise by saying: "You worked well today. You sat up in your chair, focused and followed directions. You're looking more carefully at new words and trying some different ways to identify them. When you don't understand something, you're asking for help. This is what good readers and writers do."

Do not be manipulated by the child's efforts to divert or distract you.

Variations for Flight Responses
Make sure the child is able to do what is expected. Focus on vocabulary development, comprehension and fluency as well as word recognition. Provide a "safety net" for the child when learning is difficult. Encourage the child to ask questions about the meanings of unfamiliar words and concepts. Explain by providing concrete examples, but make sure

the child transports these meanings back to the story or text and uses them to try to untangle confusions or correct misconceptions. Model positive self-talk and your thought processes as you demonstrate problem-solving behaviors.

Practice reading fluently by rehearsing unfamiliar words or sentence patterns before the child is asked to read them in a story or text. Praise and encourage approximations and nudge the child to expanded effort.

Share the pen in writing as much as needed but go slowly. Do not require too much in too short a time. Model correct spelling by writing on the practice page then ask the child to do the same. Provide opportunities for independent work using magnetic letters or charts as scaffolds. Praise the child saying: "Some of what we did today was difficult and I noticed you were a bit worried when you weren't sure what to do. But you didn't quit. You tried to help yourself by doing…, and that is what good readers and writers do."

Step 5: General Approach
Feedback and closure: Talk about specific, positive changes in the child's behavior as well as in reading and writing. Share this information with parents and other teachers.

Variations for Fight Responses
Talk with the child about appropriate and inappropriate behavior during the lesson. Ask the child to role-play appropriate coping skills and self-talk that help complete a problem-solving activity. Provide clarification and model as necessary. This approach helps a child learn how to successfully control the outcome of reading and writing instruction.

Recording positive changes in behavior, self-talk and language acquisition is as important as noting the ability to apply strategies and skills. Share this information with the child.

Occasionally, reverse roles and allow the child to teach you something during the lesson.

Variations for Flight Responses
Your role with this child is that of a coach. Lift the child, don't push. You lift by showing how to make connections between what needs to be learned and what the child knows. This is an effective approach with all children but it is especially important for those who exhibit learned helplessness or flight behaviors.

Pushing these children overwhelms them. In the face of pressure they quit or become immobilized for fear of failure or inadequacy. Your challenge is to "take baby steps" and provide scaffolds when they stumble to ensure their success so they learn to take risks.

Gradually, reduce the child's dependence on you. Record evidence of the child's independent work, risk-taking efforts, coping skills and positive changes in self-talk that are used effectively to overcome difficulty. Praise and reinforce these trials.

Occasionally you can encourage children to apply strategies and skills they have learned by using easier but unfamiliar materials. In this way, new material that is unfamiliar to the child can be successfully managed independently. This builds trust and confidence, strengthens your relationship and provides opportunities for the child to demonstrate transfer of learning, i.e., tangible evidence of the effectiveness of your teaching.

Step 6: General Approach

Setting the stage for further learning:
Review samples of the child's work to date. Talk about strengths and improvement and point out what the child needs to learn to do in the short term.

Variations for Fight Responses

Provide guidelines and previews of things to come. Give the child a clear picture of what will be done and the amount of time available to do it in the next lesson. Prepare the child for homework activities by explaining exactly how to complete them. How much or what should be done is negotiable. Then ask:

- "What do you have to do tonight?"
- "What are you going to do to finish this homework tonight?"
- "What is the purpose of you doing this?"
- "Why is this important?"
- "What are you going to bring back to me tomorrow?"
- "What can you expect if you do or do not return the materials or work?"

Explain the child's responsibility for the work being completed and returned on time. Make up a contract, read it to the child and ask for it to be signed by a parent or guardian. Be sure to "catch the child doing these things right" and reinforce the effort.

Make a point of showing the child evidence of improvement in reading and writing as well as behavior related to problem solving and independence.

Variations for Flight Responses

Work with the classroom teacher to provide the child opportunities during the day to read familiar books to a "buddy" or small group. The child can take a sealed envelope containing the "cut up" sentence from today's lesson back to the classroom. On the cover of the envelope write the sentence you and the child wrote in bold black print. Be sure to provide ample space between words and lines.

Explain to the teacher that you would like the child to write this sentence in the daily journal. The child is expected to cover the envelope with a card and begin writing. When the child is unsure of how to spell a word or which word to write, the card can be moved to expose the target letters or word. The child looks and then replaces the card while attempting to write from memory.

Limit the amount of work sent back to the classroom but ask the teacher to support the child as needed.

Show the child a record of improved performance by reviewing documented evidence and specific examples of written work. Place as much emphasis on risk-taking behavior, efforts to apply strategies, skills and independence as you do on progress in language development, reading and writing.

Step 7: General Approach

To maintain gains from intervention:

- Observe the child at work and record appropriate and inappropriate coping behaviors as well as language and literacy strategies and skills development.
- Establish a tempo that keeps the child engaged and on task. Establish and maintain a trusting relationship with the child.
- Design and implement meaningful work: When selecting books or materials in reading consider the child's interests as well as stage of oral language and concept development, known words and level of difficulty or challenge.

- Balance the amount of story reading with reading informational texts.
- Model positive self-talk and problem-solving strategies and ask the child to repeat encouraging statements to help relieve anxiety while working at point of difficulty or error.

Variations for Fight Responses

Always have backup material ready to incorporate into the lesson if what you planned to use is not successful. Being able to shift gears when working with children's fight responses is critical. This allows you to work flexibly and adjust the focus for the work, level of difficulty, interest and expectation. Your challenge is to maintain a child's engaged, time-on-task behavior, making a smooth transition from one component of the lesson to the next. Address a child's anxiety, frustration or rigidity from time to time but allow no distraction or deviation to interfere with learning.

Always emphasize the child's participation in the instructional as as well as informal conversation. Your relationship will grow out of the child's learning to regulate impulsivity or rigidity and apply strategies and skills to succeed in reading and writing. Provide appropriate reinforcement for incremental levels of improvement in the child's ability to cope with challenges as well as in language and literacy development. Establish consequences for appropriate and inappropriate behavior.

Variations for Flight Responses

Provide a flexible time schedule for children who exhibit flight responses in language and literacy development. Additional time may be needed for these children to complete some components of the lesson. Do not rush or push the child. Be quick, but don't hurry. Work to establish a tempo that allows the child enough time to complete the work but do not entertain temporizing or dilatory behavior.

Encourage children to continue working and provide explicit models of strategies and positive self-talk when necessary. Talk to them about the anxiety they may experience when things are challenging or confusing during reading and writing. Model coping behaviors and ask them to role-play these afterward.

Your relationship with these children grows out of personal conversations and shared feelings. Reinforce their efforts when learning is difficult and acknowledge and praise risk-taking behavior.

Summary

"Man can alter his life by altering his thinking." W. James

Large numbers of children are identified for special education and being learning disabled when their difficulties may be more a lack of language and literacy development (Clay, 1987).

ELL children and those with low language may experience overwhelming stress in school. They perceive language and literacy learning activities as threatening and cope using habituated, fight/flight responses. They develop a negative perception of reading and writing and of themselves as readers and writers. This makes them Hard to Reach and Hard to Teach.

Your challenge is to address not only language and literacy issues but also the counter-productive, avoidant behaviors that interfere with teaching them to read and write.

Children's anxiety is compounded by the teacher's stress responses. Successful intervention requires both you and the children to learn strategies and skills. This may involve reversing negative self-talk and learning effective coping behaviors to reduce fight/flight stress responses, i.e., frustration, anger, immobilization or learned helplessness.

10 Oracy Instruction
The Role of the School Administrator

"There is always an easy solution to every human problem, which is inevitably neat, plausible and wrong."

H.L. Mencken

Background

In this age of "accountability," administrators are besieged with mandates calling for more testing, stricter classroom controls and heightened pressure to purchase and use scripted materials specifically adopted to "increase" children's performance according to imposed standards and policies.

There is intense pressure to show improvement in all children's reading and writing achievement on state and federally mandated tests. This often leads to a "one size fits all" approach, i.e., same materials, same schedule, same standards, same tests. Despite rewarding or punishing schools and teachers for children's test results, this model of instruction leaves many children not just behind, but leaves them out (see Page 1).

Years of research demonstrate the futility of this approach. Current practice does not typically link language and literacy instruction in classrooms, thus creating widespread misunderstanding and frustration when children stall and inevitably fail (Airasian, 1988; Allington and Woodside-Jiron, 1998; Kohn, 1998).

Teachers, tutors, parents and administrators often struggle and may be at odds over how to best teach children to read and write. For a growing number of school districts, the majority of the student population consists of children learning to speak English as a second language or those whose oral language development falls behind other children of the same age.

It is impossible to work effectively with these children without changing the way teachers interact with them on a daily basis (see Figures 1 and 2, Page 2). This requires an investment in training instead of purchasing more materials. The focus in Oracy instruction is *teaching kids*, not *teaching kits*. The materials to implement Oracy instruction are already available in most schools.

There are at least four children in every classroom in this country who will not benefit from whole class instruction. Teachers need to have the time available to engage the rest of the class in meaningful learning activities so they can organize a small group of struggling language and literacy learners to work with every day for 30 minutes.

This is the only way to intensify teacher-child interactions and the only hope of changing the outcome for these children's years in school. Without reorganizing the shape of the classroom to attend directly to these

Oracy Instruction and Early Intervention: The Role of the School Administrator

children's needs in language and literacy development, they remain absent from the instructional conversation and:

- sit silently or act out;
- do not volunteer, are slow to respond during instruction and are passive toward learning;
- provide one- or two-word answers when the teacher does manage to engage them;
- spend little time each day actively involved in reading, writing and talking; and
- become progressively detached from or resistant to learning to read and write (Gentile and McMillan, 1987).

One of the worst things that can happen to a child in school is *nothing*. Traditional schooling does little to enhance these children's language and literacy development or provide them the rudder they need to navigate the increasingly demanding waters of an academic curriculum (Loban, 1976). Their oral language and literacy development is low when they start school, it remains lowest across the grades, and frequently they exit early because of basic reading and writing difficulties (Loban, 1963; Ralph, 1988; Brophy, 1990).

Children cannot learn to read and write for meaning much less accelerate their learning and "catch up" until they have control over the most common language structures and sentence transformations, vocabulary and concepts that allow them to:

- Use language/meaning cues as well as the printed text to self-monitor or solve problems they encounter while learning to read and write or while reading and writing to learn (Cummins, 1984; Clay, 1991a).
- Express themselves more explicitly and effectively, using language to make sense of those situations and intentions that interest

them (Loban, 1963; Halliday, 1973; Wells, 1987).
- Establish an oral language self-improving system that enables them to generate additional knowledge and strategies each time they engage in meaningful conversations and literacy events with a well-trained teacher (Clay, 1991).

Schools are challenged to organize and evaluate reading and writing instructional programs differently than those used traditionally (Kohn, 1999). Commercially published, or canned, skills-oriented programs do not address the development of language as the *sine qua non* of learning to read and write.

Oral language may not even be measured in school, or if it is, a single assessment is used to *evaluate* children's level of *informal conversation*. The results have limited application to the teaching of reading and writing for academic purposes because they do not guide teachers' efforts to teach children to actively participate in the *instructional conversation*.

To interact successfully with teachers and texts children must be able to formulate whole sentences as they express their thoughts, feelings and intentions. This is the foundation of learning to read and write and reading and writing to learn in school. This has significant application in schools today because as early as 1976 Loban (p. 121) said:

Oral language will remain an unimportant subject in the schools as long as it goes unevaluated. The curriculum of the language arts inevitably shrinks or expands to the boundaries of what is evaluated.

Oracy Instruction and Early Intervention: The Role of the School Administrator

Since reading and writing are language activities, it is vital for teachers to have a clear understanding of how language develops and to know the most common structures of English and how these structures are acquired by children learning to read and write.

This knowledge helps teachers interact more effectively in order to expand and refine children's language and use the results of the three forms of the OLAI to demonstrate growth over time.

Working with Teachers to Develop a School-wide Oracy Instructional Curriculum

Following are some of the ways school administrators can foster the development of an Oracy instructional curriculum school-wide to support make-up opportunities for ELLs and those with low oral language development.

1. Create an Oracy Instructional Team (OIT). Elect one representative for each grade. The representative meets with you and others involved in the literacy program (the curriculum director, the literacy coordinator and literacy coaches or leaders) to establish clear, reachable goals for integrating Oracy instruction in every classroom.

2. Ask teachers to complete the Survey of Language and Literacy Instruction (see Appendix A, Page 84) to determine the following:
   • What exactly is being taught?
   • How much language and literacy is being taught at each grade level and in each classroom?
   • How much of what you and the OIT agree upon as the goals for your school or district are being addressed?
   • How are language development and literacy being measured?
   • Which materials or books are being used to teach language and literacy?
   • How is language and literacy instruction included in each teacher's daily lesson plan?
   • How many opportunities does the teacher provide for children to talk about what is read to them or what they view in videos or listen to on audiotapes?
   • How much time do children spend reading and writing independently, and how much talking do they do with the teacher or each other while learning to read and write or while reading and writing to learn?

3. Visit classrooms during the language arts instructional block. Use the Classroom Observation Form (see Appendix B, Page 87) to evaluate language and literacy instruction. Later, compare the results of the teacher survey with your observations. Review the results with the OIT and the teachers individually or in a group. Make recommendations for designing and implementing Oracy instruction.

4. Using the form in Appendix C (see Closing the Gap: Observation Guide, Page 88), compare the instruction provided to one child at or above grade level in language and literacy learning with the instruction provided to one of the lowest performing children in a classroom. Review the results of these observations with the OIT and the teachers and incorporate them in your plan.

5. Require the use of the OLAI to measure children's oral language development and have teachers use the results to design and deliver effective Oracy instruction.

6. Encourage teachers to set aside time each

day to work with four struggling language and literacy learners in a small group to provide Oracy instruction.

7. Support teachers' efforts to spend time with children, talking about things every day in the physical and social world and listening and prompting for expansions and refinements of language structures, vocabulary and concepts.

8. Encourage the involvement and training of aides, volunteers and parents to provide assistance to classroom teachers in support of language and literacy development.

9. Foster a school-wide climate that encourages staff, faculty and children to become involved and interact every day with children in ways that promote language development.

10. Encourage your local school board to develop policies that support these efforts and involve the entire community.

The Oracy Instructional Design

Oracy instruction links language and literacy development using the evidence-based interactive components of the OLAI (see pages 11-15).

- **Component I. Repeated Sentences:** Restating, expanding and refining children's responses.

- **Component II. Story Reconstruction and Narrative Comprehension:** Learning to code information using two sources, i.e., pictures and language to create and narrate a story.

- **Component III. Picture Drawing, Narration and Dictation:** Combining language development and action (activity) and demonstrating processing strategies, i.e., reading and writing and phonemic awareness, i.e., hearing and identifying sounds in words.

- **Component IV. Information Processing and Critical Dialogue:** Demonstrating a "threshold stage" of academic language development and content interpretation.

Philosophy and Practice

1. Administrative support: Faculty and staff training, targeted systemic intervention across the grades (classroom and tutorial).

2. Individual assessment over time to identify the "most common language structures" children need to control to read and write classroom texts: Components of assessment linked directly to instruction emphasizing teaching interactions to shape children's oral, expressive language as well as self-talk and body language.

3. Small group instruction of four children: Learning by doing. Teachers interact with children, eliciting and restating responses to expand and refine their oral language.

4. Developing Oracy charts: Incorporating expanded and refined structures and vocabulary to teach reading and writing processing strategies, i.e., learning how text works.

5. Tiered instruction: Gradually increasing the levels of challenge in reading and writing to employ an array of commercially published materials and activities that educate and entertain, i.e., teach children how the world works.

6. Parents, family members and caregivers: Training to provide specific interactions at home to support the work of teachers in the classroom.

Oracy Instruction and Early Intervention: The Role of the School Administrator

II Oracy Instruction
The Role of Parents and Caregivers

"Children must learn to listen, speak, read and write. Cognition research and infant development studies show that 'early language stimulation—from the moment of birth—influences brain development and later learning success.'"

(A. Lewis, 1996)

Fixing the schools is not enough (Ogbu, 2002). Parents and caregivers are children's first teachers and play a critical role in shaping language and literacy development. Changing the way parents and caregivers interact with children is essential to children's learning and success in school.

But, many of these people live in poverty, lack formal education and do not speak English or are functionally illiterate. They lead stressful lives. They want the best for their children but do not know what to do to help that does not require a broad knowledge or understanding of instructional practice. They are concerned about doing something wrong or interfering with the school. If they do not speak English they may not see the value of interacting with children in their native language or understand that talk is the bedrock of literacy.

Parents and caregivers can benefit from practical training to broaden and intensify interactions with children using activities based on the components of *The Oral Language Acquisition Inventory*. These do not require them to be literate. They can supplement this work using skills they possess from their jobs or individual talents, i.e., agriculture, mechanical, industrial or construction trades, housekeeping, cooking, sewing, storytelling, art, music, drama, dance or crafts.

Parents and caregivers need specific examples to show not only *what* they can do and *how* to do it, but *why* it is important (see Figure 7, Page 78). They need demonstrations of helpful ways to change the interactions they have with children. These interactions form the foundation that supports learning how to respond successfully to teachers and instruction at school (see pages 16-17).

Components

Component I:
Repeated Sentences Activity
Learning how to engage children in a meaningful conversation is the first step in

Figure 7
Oracy Instruction: A Model for Parents and Caregivers

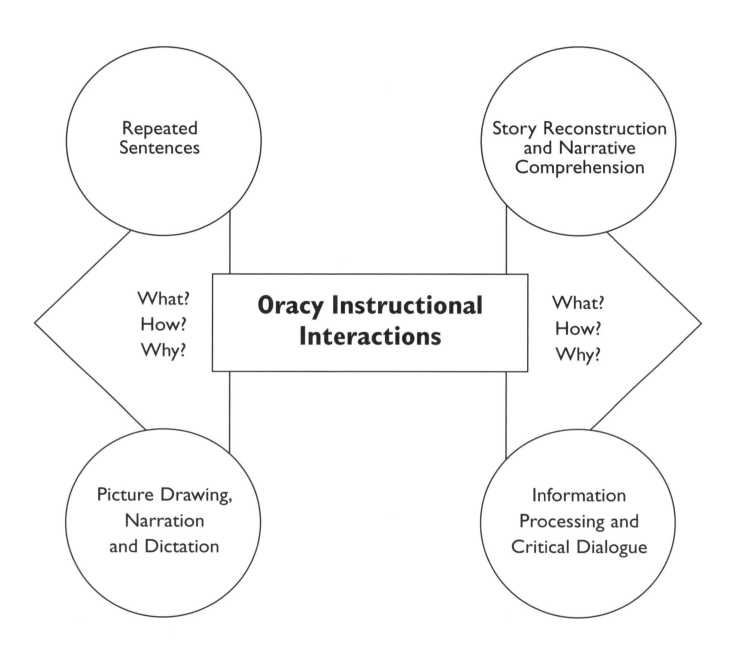

Repeated Sentences

Story Reconstruction and Narrative Comprehension

What?
How?
Why?

Oracy Instructional Interactions

What?
How?
Why?

Picture Drawing, Narration and Dictation

Information Processing and Critical Dialogue

helping parents and caregivers understand the importance of language in learning to read and write. This seems obvious, but many children's interactions are characterized by having to respond to command, criticism or threat. They can help children acquire language needed to read and write in school by using complete sentences in conversations with them and encouraging children to do the same.

Some adults have only had experience talking *at* children and have to be shown how to talk *with* them. There are some key things to do to engage a child in meaningful conversation. Parents and caregivers can learn to:

- Listen, wait for children to respond and not interrupt.
- Try to look at children face-to-face when talking with them and pay close attention to what they are saying.
- Show understanding and empathy and invite children to say more.

Simply smiling and nodding in agreement can be enough to encourage a child to continue.

Adults can practice ways of engaging children and eliciting information from them beyond asking literal questions by learning to say: "Tell me more about that." "That's interesting. I didn't know that." "Can you say more about it?"

Learning how to restate what children say, expand or add to their responses and using different words to clarify or brighten a conversation is at the heart of helping children interact with teachers and instructional materials in school.

Component II: Story Reconstruction and Narrative Comprehension Activity

The ability of children to look at three or four pictures and put them in order to tell a logically sequenced story links language and literacy development. It is important to show parents and caregivers how to cut out pictures from the comic section of a newspaper or magazine, paste them on pieces of stiff paper or cardboard and tell stories about them. They have to demonstrate for children how to tell a story using picture frames first and then invite them to use the pictures to tell "their story."

Parents and caregivers can be shown how to string a piece of cord or rope across a doorway and, using a clothespin, attach each picture while they describe the activity or conversation sequenced in each picture. Then invite children to "tell the story." Afterwards, they remove the pictures from the line, hand them to the child and allow the child to "tell a story," pinning the pictures in a logical sequence back on the line. They can also lay the pictures out on a tabletop as they narrate a related story, then shuffle the pictures and ask the child to reorganize them to tell a story.

This lays the foundation for children learning how to organize information using language and pictures, to not only tell a story, but also to talk about what they may have learned in relation to content area subject matter. Parents and caregivers are encouraged to use the same set of pictures several times, adding more details to the story or information as they retell it or talk about it each time. Ultimately, children should be able to sequence the pictures to tell their own story or provide information they have learned from the pictures and narrative containing expanded details.

Component III: Picture Drawing, Narration and Dictation Activity (Puzzles)

Parents and caregivers can motivate children to draw either independently or by sharing the drawing in ways that encourage them to talk. This activity develops children's ability to look, see, listen, coordinate hand-eye movements and communicate their thoughts, feelings and intentions.

Drawing and talking about what they draw develops children's visual and auditory perception and spatial organization. These strengths support their learning to identify differences among sounds and letters and symbols that appear on a written page. Drawing also requires children to learn where to begin working on a page, where to finish, how to control a marker or pen and the movements needed to create shapes and patterns. Distinguishing between shapes and patterns is the essence of letter formation and early reading and writing.

Parents and caregivers who draw with children and talk about their drawings help them learn to divide their attention as they interact with the activity and them. They learn to take turns while talking and answering or asking questions. These are some of the most important things they have to do to respond effectively to teachers and texts in the classroom.

Showing parents and caregivers how to assemble puzzles and *talk* with children while working with them also supports concentration and focus, taking risks, making predictions, coordinating hand-eye movements and applying different strategies to solve problems when they are confused or stuck.

Component IV: Information Processing and Critical Dialogue

Parents and caregivers can learn to watch portions of informational videos or television programs and interact with children to develop meaningful conversations. Asking children questions about a video or television segment and helping them fill in the blanks or provide details, i.e., "Who?" "What?" "When?" "Where?" "How?" or "Why?" promotes children's vocabulary development and comprehension and their ability to talk about content material.

They can also learn to ask open-ended questions and invite conversation by saying: "Tell me one important thing you learned about…" "Tell me what you were thinking while we watched…" "Tell me what you were feeling." "Tell me the most important question you might ask about…" "Tell me about something or someone you know like…" If children cannot respond, parents and caregivers can learn how to model their own thoughts or provide clear examples for them. These interactions help children acquire the language of emotion as well as instruction.

Learning to identify important facts and main ideas as well as storing, retrieving and analyzing information are skills required across the grades. But children have to learn how to talk about and interpret information based on their own thinking and feelings as well. Through Critical Dialogues they learn how to pose questions or define the most significant things they learn from reading and writing activities and connect what they learn to something in their personal lives. These dialogues help clarify, confirm or refute what they know and have the power to transform language and behavior.

The components of the OLAI provide a structure for training parents and caregivers to work with children for these purposes. While some may not feel they have the time or background to support children's language and literacy development, they can do these things in different settings, at different times during the course of the day.

Conversations with children can occur anywhere at any time using any one of the contexts or activities that form the structure of the OLAI.

Without consistent parental or caregiver support the effect of what is done in school to help ELL children and those struggling to acquire language and literacy "catch up" is confined to the limited interactions that take place in a classroom. This is not enough to overcome the barriers to these children's learning.

Instead of excuses and apologies or blame, they need targeted intervention at home, at school and across the grades. This requires a systemic change in the way these children are taught, the way classrooms are organized and the way schools, parents and caregivers are involved.

12 A Final Word

*"We shall not cease from exploration/And the end of all our exploring/
Will be to arrive where we started/And know the place for the first time."*

T.S. Eliot

The challenges of working with children who require specific attention in language and literacy development are complex and demanding. There may be many reasons children need extra assistance. Some may require referral for other services.

It takes time to teach children who are struggling to develop oral language and those acquiring a second language. They can become literate and succeed in school if the inordinate amount of nonproductive time already spent on them is reorganized.

> **Clay (1997, p.204) said:**
>
> *Low achievement may arise from lack of learning opportunities, or because the child chose to attend to other things, or because the child has the fine motor skill and language level of a much younger child. Life events and crises in the preschool or early school years may also contribute to low achievement. If the learner is to read and write, every attempt must be made to help the child attend to basic literacy responses.*

Thirty minutes of daily Oracy instruction can help children develop a "threshold of linguistic proficiency" (Cummins, 1984) or "self extending oral language system" (Clay, 1991). This involves children in planned listening, speaking, reading, writing and viewing activities designed to get them talking and participating in instructional conversations. Among the differences that have been found between high achieving and low achieving children are: 1) amount of reading and writing done each day, 2) time spent reading and writing, 3) access to a wide variety of written material, and 4) good language and literacy instruction (Allington, 1995; Krashen, 1995).

The research on extensive reading and writing shows not only language learning gains from these activities but social and affective benefits as well (Fillmore, 1979; Elley, 1991).

Children become confident readers and writers when they acquire language in a meaningful context and are taught specific strategies to cope successfully when they encounter difficulty with schoolwork. Ironically, while there is evidence that many children struggling with language development lack self-confidence when it comes to reading and writing, much of what they experience in school compounds their problems. Extensive, recursive teaching of literacy skills may actually produce a loss in confidence and achievement (Gentile and McMillan, 1987a, 1987b).

Once children control the most common language structures and can transform sentences in their oral speech, further development is dependent on three types of ongoing, intensified interactions and opportunities to:

- Hear a higher register of language used by adults in conversations they have with them while expressing thoughts and feelings.
- Experiment with language, using a variety of structures and vocabulary in meaningful conversations.
- Read and write more challenging texts.

We can further shape the development of literacy skills by *talking* during the creative process as well as reading, writing and *talking* about texts that are rich in vocabulary and concepts.

Oral language cannot be scripted; it is caught more than taught, acquired and inspired through a child's consistent interactions and conversations with those who are fluent in the language.

Testing and retesting in literacy without evaluating growth in language and incorporating the results in teaching both limits and can damage children's motivation to learn.

Unless early systemic intervention is initiated for children entering school with low language and literacy development, most of them will inevitably drop out or be pushed out of school because of basic reading and writing difficulties (Ralph, 1988). They will not develop "literate minds" (Dorn and Soffos, 2001) and will not use education to invent their futures. Feurstein (1980) said: "It is possible to have a brain and not have a mind. A brain is inherited; a mind is developed" (see Figure 8).

Someone once said, "Vision without action is just a dream; action without vision is a waste of time; vision combined with action can change lives." Putting language development first and using the OLAI to link language and literacy learning and to design and implement daily Oracy instruction can change the outcome of schooling for these children and their families.

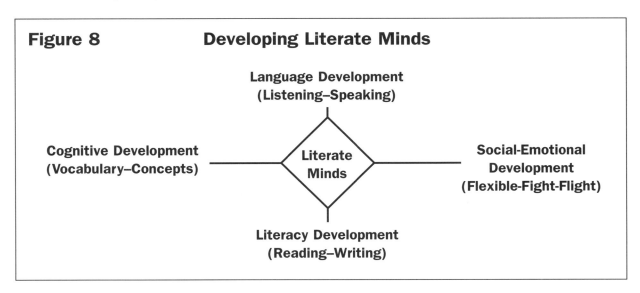

Figure 8   Developing Literate Minds

Language Development
(Listening–Speaking)

Cognitive Development
(Vocabulary–Concepts)

Literate Minds

Social-Emotional
Development
(Flexible-Fight-Flight)

Literacy Development
(Reading–Writing)

Appendix

A Survey of Language and Literacy Instruction

To Be Completed by Classroom Teacher

Listening and Speaking

Each day, children are given an opportunity to:

1. **Identify letters and sounds in words in meaningful contexts through planned instruction.**
   Activity and materials used:

   _____

   _____

   _____

   Number of minutes each day:
   5 10 15 20 25 30 40 45 50 55 60

2. **Listen to a story and talk about it for planned purposes.**
   The story can be told, read, or be in the form of a video or other media.
   Activity and materials used:

   _____

   _____

   _____

   Number of minutes each day:
   5 10 15 20 25 30 40 45 50 55 60

3. **Listen to a nonfiction selection read by the teacher, and talk about it for planned purposes.**
   Activity and materials used:

   _____

   _____

   _____

   Number of minutes each day:
   5 10 15 20 25 30 40 45 50 55 60

Reading

Each day, children are given an opportunity to:

1. Read stories containing common language structures and talk about them.

Activity and materials used:

_____

_____

_____

Number of minutes each day:
5 10 15 20 25 30 40 45 50 55 60

2. Learn vocabulary and apply word knowledge during guided, shared, or independent reading for planned purposes.

Activity and materials used:

_____

_____

_____

Number of minutes each day:
5 10 15 20 25 30 40 45 50 55 60

3. Learn concepts about print (CAP), looking at print (LAPS) and problem-solving strategies.

Activity and materials used:

_____

_____

_____

Number of minutes each day:
5 10 15 20 25 30 40 45 50 55 60

4. Develop comprehension strategies from planned instruction.

Activity and materials used:

_____

_____

_____

Number of minutes each day:
5 10 15 20 25 30 40 45 50 55 60

The Oracy Instructional Guide 85

(This page may be reproduced for classroom use.) Appendix A

5. Read independently for planned purposes and talk about what they've read.

Activity and materials used:

_____

_____

_____

Number of minutes each day:
5 10 15 20 25 30 40 45 50 55 60

Writing

Each day, children are given an opportunity to:

1. Do shared writing with a teacher or other children for planned purposes.

Activity and materials used:

_____

_____

_____

Number of minutes each day:
5 10 15 20 25 30 40 45 50 55 60

2 Write independently for planned purposes.

Activity and materials used:

_____

_____

_____

Number of minutes each day:
5 10 15 20 25 30 40 45 50 55 60

3. Read what they write to a teacher or other children and talk about what they've written.

Activity and materials used:

_____

_____

_____

Number of minutes each day:
5 10 15 20 25 30 40 45 50 55 60

The Oracy Instructional Guide

Appendix A (This page may be reproduced for classroom use.)

Classroom Language and Literacy Instruction

Classroom Observation Form

(Check what you observe. Write comments on back.)

Interactions

____ Teacher consistently encourages children to talk.

____ Teacher encourages all children to participate.

____ Teacher groups children for varied purposes, using planned language and literacy learning activities.

____ Teacher provides opportunities for shared, guided and independent reading and writing.

____ Teacher provides a "print rich" environment. (Children's writing on display, photographs/pictures with appropriate labels or accompanying text, labels throughout the room, maps, principles related to skills or strategies in literacy, motivational sayings, classroom rules, etc.

____ The classroom contains instructional materials. (Easel, felt board, butcher paper, big books, an assortment of fiction and nonfiction books, videos and audiotapes, children's individual baskets containing familiar books, writing tablets, markers, etc.)

____ Teacher's lesson plan includes specific language and literacy instructional activities, i.e., readers'/writers' workshop, dictation charts, guided/shared or independent reading and writing.

____ Teacher models appropriate literacy behaviors. (Concepts about print, looking at print, problem-solving strategies, hearing and recording sounds in words, think-alouds, etc.)

____ Teacher reads to and talks with children about content, vocabulary, and concepts. Facilitates, rather than controls, conversation.

The Oracy Instructional Guide 87

(This page may be reproduced for classroom use.) Appendix B

Appendix

Closing the Gap
Observation Guide

Observe two children during the language arts instructional block. Identify one child who is achieving at or above grade level (Child #1), and one of the lowest performing children (Child #2). Record your observations and comments.

Child #1

_____

Child Volunteers

_____

Teacher-Child Interactions

_____

Child Talks

_____

Child Reads/Writes Independently

Child #2

_____

Child Volunteers

_____

Teacher-Child Interactions

_____

Child Talks

_____

Child Reads/Writes Independently

The Oracy Instructional Guide

Appendix C (This page may be reproduced for classroom use.)

References

Airaisan, P. (1988). Measurement driven instruction: A closer look. *Educational Measurement: Issues and Practice, 7*, (4), 6-11.

Allen, R.V. (1976). *Language experiences in communication.* Boston: Houghton Mifflin.

Allington, R.L. (1995). Flunking: Throwing good money after bad. In *No quick fix: Rethinking literacy programs in America's elementary schools.* Allington, R.L. and Walmsley S.A. (Eds.), New York: Teachers College Press.

Allington, R.L. and Woodside-Jiron, H. (1998). Thirty years of research in reading: When is a research summary not a research summary. In *In defense of good teaching: What teachers need to know about the "Reading Wars."* (Ed.), K. Goodman. York, ME: Stenhouse.

Allington, R.L. and Cunningham, P. (1998). *Classrooms that work.* New York: Longman.

Askew, B. and Fountas, I. (1997). Active from the start. *The Running Record, 9,* (1), 1-13.

Bandura, A. (1977). *Social learning theory.* Englewood Cliffs, NJ: Prentice-Hall.

Bandura A. and Cervone, D. (1984). *Differential engagement of self-reactive influences in motivation.* Unpublished manuscript, Stanford University.

Bandura, A. (January, 1985). *Social learning theory.* Paper presented at the Carnegie Conference on Unhealthful risk-taking behavior in adolescence, San Francisco.

Bernstein, L. E. (1981). Language as a product of dialogue. *Discourse Practices, 4,* 117-147.

Bissex, G. (1980). *Gnys at wrk: A child learns to write and read.* Cambridge, MA: Harvard University Press.

Blachman, B. (1984). Language analysis skills and early reading acquisition. In G. Wallace and K. Butler (Eds.), *Language learning disabilities in school-age children* (pp. 271-287). Baltimore: Williams and Wilkins.

Blachman, G.J. and Silberman, A. (1980). *Modification of child and adolescent behavior.* Belmont, CA: Wadsworth Publishing.

Blakemore, C.J. and Ramirez, B.W. (1999). *Literacy centers for the primary classroom.* Carlsbad, CA: Dominie Press, Inc.

Brabham, E.G. and Villaume, S.K. (November, 2002). Vocabulary instruction: Concerns and visions. *The Reading Teacher, 55,* (3), 264-267.

Brookes, M. (1986). *Drawing with children.* New York: St. Martin's Press.

Brophy, J.E. (1990). Effective schooling for disadvantaged students. In M.S. Knapp and P.M. Shields (Eds.), *Better schooling for the children of poverty: Alternatives to conventional wisdom* (Vol. 2, pp. 1-26). Washington, D.C.: U.S. Department of Education.

Brown, J.S., Collins, A. and Duguid, (1989, February). Situated cognition and the culture of learning. *Educational Researcher, 18,* 32.

Bruner, J. (1983). *Child's talk: Learning to use language.* London: W.W. Norton and Co.

Brunn, M. (2002). The four-square strategy. *The Reading Teacher, 55,* (6), 522-525.

Byrne, B.W. (1984). The general/academic self concept nomological network. *Review of Educational Research*, 54, 450.

Calkins, L. (1986). *The art of teaching writing.* Portsmouth, NH: Heinemann.

Chamot, A.U. and O'Malley, J.M. (1989). The cognitive academic language learning approach. In P. Rigg and V.G. Allen (Eds.), *When they can't all speak English: Integrating the ESL student into the regular classroom.* National Council Teachers of English.

Clay, M.M. (1971). Juncture, pitch and stress as reading behaviour variables. *Journal of Verbal Behaviour and Verbal Learning*, 10: 133-139.

Clay, M.M. (1975). *What did I write?* Auckland, NZ: Heinemann.

Clay, M.M., Gill, M., Glynn, T., McNaughton, T. and Salmon, K. (1983). *The record of oral language and biks and gutches.* Auckland, NZ: Heinemann.

Clay, M.M. (1986). Learning to be learning disabled. *New Zealand Journal of Educational Studies*, 22, (2), 155-173.

Clay, M.M. (1989, January). Concepts about print in English and other languages. *The Reading Teacher*, 268-276.

Clay, M.M. (1991a). *Becoming literate. The construction of inner control.* Portsmouth, NH: Heinemann.

Clay, M.M. (1991b). Introducing a new storybook to young readers. *The Reading Teacher.* 45, 264-273.

Clay, M. (1993). *An observation survey of early literacy achievement.* Portsmouth, NH: Heinemann.

Clay, M. (2002). *An observation survey of early literacy achievement* (2nd. ed.). Portsmouth, NH: Heinemann.

Clay, M. (1995). *A guidebook for Reading Recovery teachers in training.* Portsmouth, NH: Heinemann.

Clay, M. (1998). *By different paths to common outcomes.* York, ME: Stenhouse.

Clay, M. (2001). *Change over time in children's literacy development* (pp. 23-31). Portsmouth, NH: Heinemann.

Combs, M. (1987). Modeling the reading process with enlarged texts. *The Reading Teacher*, 40, 422-426.

Cummins, J. (1984). Underachievement among minority students. *Bilingualism and Special Education.* Avon: England. Multilingual Matters, Ltd.

Cummins, J. (1995). Underachievement among minority students. In D.B. Durkin (Ed.). *Language issues* (pp. 130-159). White Plains, NY: Longman.

Cunningham, P.M. (1995). *Phonics they use: Words for reading and writing.* (2nd ed.) New York: Harper Collins.

Deci, E.L. Spiegel, N.H., Ryan, R.M, Foestner, R. and Kaufman, M. (1982). Effects of performance standards on teaching styles: Behavior of controlling teachers. *Journal of Educational Psychology*, 74, (6), 852-859.

Deci, E.L. (March, 1985). The well-tempered classroom – how not to motivate teachers and students: Impose stricter standards, more controls and greater conformity. *Psychology Today*, 52-53.

Dorn, L. and Soffos, C. (2001). *Shaping literate minds.* Portland, ME: Stenhouse.

DuCharme, C.C. (1996, Winter). Drawing to write: The role of drawing in the writing processes of kindergarten and primary grade children. *Kindergarten Education*, 1(2), 54-61.

Duffy, G., Roehler, L. and Hermann, B. (1988). Modeling mental processes helps poor readers become more strategic readers. *The Reading Teacher*, 42, 762-767.

Durkin, D. (1995). Developing literacy. In D. Durkin (Ed.), *Language issues*, (p.405). White Plains, NY: Longman.

Dyson, A.H. (1986). Transitions and tensions: Interrelationships between the drawing, talking and dictating of young children. *Research in the Teaching of English*, 20, 379-409.

Elkonin, D.B. (1971). Development of Speech. In A.Z. Zaporozhets and D.B. Elkonin (Eds.) The psychology of preschool children. Kindergarten Children, 1 (2:54-61).

Elley, W.B. and Magubahai, F. (1981a). *The impact of a book flood in Fiji primary schools*. Wellington, NZCER.

Elley, W.B. and Mangubahai, F. (1981b). The long-term effects of a book flood on children's language growth. *Directions*, 7, 15-24.

Elley, W.B. (1989). Vocabulary acquisition from listening to stories. *Reading Research Quarterly*, 24, (2), 174-187.

Fennessy, S. (1995). Living history through drama and literature. *The Reading Teacher*, 49, 16-19.

Feurstein, R. (1980). *Instrumental enrichment: An intervention program for cognitive modifiability*. Glenview, IL: Scott Foresman & Co.

Ford, M.P. (1991). Worksheets anonymous: On the road to recovery. *Language Arts*, 6, 553-559.

Ford, M.P. (1996). Tightening up: Working toward balanced literacy. *The Whole Idea*, 7, (1), 12-15.

Ford, M.P. and Opitz, M.F. (May, 2002). Using centers to engage children during guided reading time: Intensifying learning experiences away from the teacher. *The Reading Teacher*, 55, (8), 710-717.

Fountas, I. and Pinnell, G.S. (1996). *Guided reading. Good first teaching for all children*. Portsmouth, NH: Heinemann.

Fountas, I. and Pinnell, G.S. (2001). *Guiding readers and writers: Grades 3-6*. Portsmouth, NH: Heinemann.

Gallagher, J.M. (1996, Winter). Piaget's symbolic function and the foundation of reading. *Kindergarten Education: Theory, Research and Practice*, 1, (2), 54-61.

Gentile, L.M., McMillan, M. and Swain, C. (1985). Parents' identification of children's life crises: Stress as a factor in reading difficulties. In G.H. McNinch (Ed.), Reading Research in 1984: Comprehension, computers, communication. *Fifth Yearbook of the American Reading Forum*. Carrollton, GA: Thomasson Printing and Office Equipment.

Gentile, L.M. and McMillan, M. (1987a). *Stress and reading difficulties: Research, assessment and intervention*. Newark, DE: International Reading Association.

Gentile, L.M. and McMillan, M. (1987b). Stress and reading difficulties: Teaching students self regulating skills. *The Reading Teacher*, 41, 170-178.

Gentile, L.M. and McMillan, M. (1990). Literacy through literature. Motivating at risk students to read and write. *Journal of Reading, Writing and Learning Disabilities International*, 6, 383-393.

Gentile, L.M. and McMillan, M. (1991, Spring). Literacy for at risk students: The relationship between student and teacher. *School of Education Review*. San Francisco: San Francisco State University.

Gentile, L.M. and McMillan, M. (1992). Literacy for students at risk: Developing critical dialogues. *The Journal of Reading*, 35, (8), 636-641.

Gentile, L.M. and McMillan, M. (1994, March). Critical dialogue: The road to literacy for students at risk in middle schools. *Middle School Journal*, 50-54.

Gentile, L. M. and McMillan, M. (1995). Critical dialogue: A literacy curriculum for students at risk in the middle grades. *Reading and Writing Quarterly*. 11, 123-136.

Gentile, L.M. (1997). Oral language assessment and development in reading recovery in the United States. In S. Schwartz and A. Klein (Eds.), *Research in reading recovery*. Portsmouth, NH: Heinemann.

Gentile, L.M. (2001). The identification and comparison of children's language structures used by Reading Recovery children who did and did not discontinue in twenty weeks. *Research paper presented to the Third North American Leadership Academy*, Washington, D.C.

Gentile, L.M. (2003). *Monograph: The research base for developing The Oral Language Acquisition Inventory*. Carlsbad, CA: Dominie Press, Inc.

Glasswell, K., Parr, M. and McNaughton, S. (2003). Working with William: Teaching, learning and the joint construction of a struggling writer. *The Reading Teacher*, 56, (5), 494-500.

Goldenberg, C. (1993). Instructional conversations: Promoting comprehension through discussion. *The Reading Teacher*, 46 (4): 316-326.

Good, R.H., Kaminski, R. and Smith, S. (2001). Phoneme segmentation fluency. In Good, R.H. and Kaminski, R.A. (Eds.), *Dynamic Indicators of Basic Early Literacy Skills*, (5th ed.), Eugene, OR: Institute for the Development of Educational Achievement.

Goodlad, J. (1984). *A place called school*. New York: McGraw-Hill.

Grant, R.A. and Wong, S.D. (February, 2003). Barriers to literacy for language minority learners: An argument for change in the literacy education profession. *Journal of Adolescent and Adult Literacy*, 48, (5), 386-394.

Graves, D. (1983). *Writing: Teachers and children at work*. Exeter, NH: Heinemann.

Gray, B. (1984). *Helping children to become language learners in the classroom*. Darwin, Australia: Northern Territory Department of Education.

Greenspan, S. and Lodish, R. (1992). School literacy: The real ABCs. *Phi Delta Kappan*, 72, 300-308.

Hall-Bedrova, E. and Leong, D.J. (1996). *Tools of the mind* (pp. 108-120). Columbus, OH: Merrill.

Halliday, M.A.K. (1973). *Learning how to mean: Explorations in the development of language*. London: Edward Arnold.

Hanf-Buckley, M. (1992, December). Focus on research: We listen a book a day; We speak a book a week: Learning from Walter Loban. *Language Arts*, 69, 622-626.

Healy, J.M. (1991). *Endangered minds: Why our children don't think*. New York: Touchstone Books.

Healy, J.M. (1999). *Failure to connect*. New York: Touchstone Books.

Hilgard, E.R., Atkinson, R.C. and Atkinson, R.L. (1975). *Introduction to psychology*. New York: Harcourt Brace Jovanovich.

Holdaway, D. (1981). Shared book experience: Teaching reading using favorite books. *Theory into Practice*, 21, 293-300.

Horn, J.C. (1986). Pumping iron, pumping ego. *Psychology Today*, 20, 16.

Hudelson, S. (1994). Literacy development of second language children. In F. Genesee (Ed.). *Educating second language children*. New York: Cambridge University Press.

Jewell, T.A. and Pratt, D. (1999). Literature discussions in the primary grades: Children's thoughtful discourse about books and what teachers can do to make it happen. *The Reading Teacher*, 52, 842-849.

Kane, K. and Klein, A. (1995). *Wonder world on stage: Interpretation and performance*. Lands End Publishing, Lower Hutt: New Zealand.

Kanfer, F.H. (1980). Self management methods. In F.H. Kanfer and P. Goldstein (Eds.), *Helping people change: A textbook of methods*. New York: Pergamon Press.

Keenan, E.O. (1977). Making it last. Repetition in children's discourse. In S.E. Tripp and C. Mitchell-Kernan (Eds.), *Child Discourse*, San Diego, CA: Academic Press.

Keene, E.O. and Zimmermann, S. (1997). *Mosaic of thought*. Portsmouth, NH: Heinemann.

Kohn, A. (1998). *What to look for in a classroom*. New York: John Wiley and Sons.

Kohn, A. (1999). *The schools our children deserve: Moving beyond traditional standards and "tougher standards."* New York: Houghton Mifflin.

Krashen, S. (1995). Bilingual Education and Second Language Acquisition Theory. In D.B. Durkin (Ed.), *Language issues: Readings for teachers*. White Plains, NY: Longman.

Langer, J., Bartolome, L., Vasquez, O. and Lucas, T. (1990). Line-by-line protocol. *American Education Research Journal*, 27, (3), 427-471.

Lewis, A.C. (November 1996). *Breaking the culture of poverty*. Phi Delta Kappan, 78 (3), 186-187.

Loban, W. (1963). The language of elementary school children. *(NCTE Research Report No. 1)*. Urbana, IL: National Council Teachers of English.

Loban, W. (1976). Teaching language and literature: Grades seven-twelve *(NCTE Research Report No. 18)*. Urbana, IL: National Council Teachers of English.

Luria, A.R. (1968). The role of speech in the formation of temporary connections and the regulation of behavior in the normal and oligophrenic child. In B. Simon and J. Simon, (Eds.), *Educational Psychology in the USSR*. Stanford, CA: Stanford University Press.

Luria, A.R. (1976). *Cognitive development: Its cultural and social foundations*. (M. Lopez-Morillas and L. Solotaroff, Trans.). Cambridge, MA: Harvard University Press.

Lyons, C. (1999). Emotions, cognition and becoming a reader: A message to teachers of struggling learners. *Literacy Teaching and Learning*, 4, (1), 67-87.

Mann, V.A. (1991). Phonological abilities: Effective Predictors of future reading ability. In L. Rieben and C.A. Perfetti (Eds.), *Learning to read: Basic research and its implications* (pp. 121-133). Hillsdale, NJ: Lawrence Erlbaum.

Manzo, A. (1987). Psychologically induced dyslexia and learning disabilities. *The Reading Teacher*, 40, (4), 408-413.

Marsh, H.W., Byrne, B.M. and Shavelson, R.J. (1988). A multifaceted academic self concept. *Journal of Educational Psychology*, 80, 366-380.

McNaughton, S. (1995). *Patterns of emergent literacy: Processes of development and transition.* Melbourne, Vic, Australia: Oxford University Press.

Meadows, G. and Vial, C. (2003). *Spiders & Scorpions.* Carlsbad, CA: Dominie Press, Inc.

Moll, L. (1980). Social and instructional issues in educating disadvantaged students. In M.S. Knapp and P.M. Shields (Eds.), *Better schooling for the children of poverty: Alternatives to conventional wisdom* (Vol. 1, pp.1-22). Washington, D.C.: U.S. Office of Education.

Monroe, M. (1965). Necessary preschool experiences for comprehending reading. *Proceedings of the Ninth Annual Convention of the International Reading Association,* Vol.10, (pp.45-46), Newark, DE: International Reading Association.

Moore, K.B. (2001, October). How are you introducing literacy in your program? *Early Childhood Today.* 16, (2), 8-9.

Morrow, L. (1997). *The literacy center: Contexts for reading and writing.* York, ME: Stenhouse Publishers.

National Reading Panel Report. (2000). *Teaching children to read: An evidence-based assessment of the scientific research literature on reading and its implications for reading instruction.* Washington, D.C.: National Institute of Child Health and Human Development.

NCLB (No Child Left Behind, 2000). U.S. Department of Education legislation. Washington, D.C.

Nelson, O.G. and Linek, W.M. (1999). *Practical classroom applications of language experience.* Boston: Allyn and Bacon.

Neuman, S.B., Copple, C. and Bredekamp, S. (2000). *Learning to Read and Write: Developmentally appropriate practices for young children.* National Association for Young Children.

Ogbu, J. (2003). *Black American students in an affluent suburb: A study of academic disengagement.* Mahawah, NJ: LEA Publishers.

Ogle, D. (1986). K-W-L: A teaching model that develops active reading of expository text. *The Reading Teacher*, 39, 564-570.

Perry, B.D. (1997). Incubated in terror: Neurodevelopmental factors in the "cycle of violence." In J. Osofsky (Ed.), *Children, youth and violence: The search for solutions.* New York: Guilford Press, 124-148.

Perry, B.D. and Azad, I. (1999). Post-traumatic stress disorders in children and adolescents. *Current Opinion in Pediatrics*, 11, 121-132.

Pickard, N. (1996). Out of class language learning strategies. *ELT Journal*, 50(2), 150-159.

Pinker, S. (1994). *The language instinct: How the mind creates language.* New York: William Morrow.